The Power of Self

The Key to Confidence

The Power of Self Hypnosis –

The Key to Confidence
Gilbert Oakley

foulsham
LONDON • NEW YORK • TORONTO • SYDNEY

foulsham

Bennetts Close, Cippenham, Berkshire, SL1 5AP

ISBN 0–572–01135–0

Copyright © 1989 W. Foulsham and Co. Ltd.

Printed in Great Britain at St Edmundsbury Press,

Contents

Introduction

It was Emile Coué (1857–1926) a French pharmacist, who first introduced the technique of auto-suggestion and self-hypnosis by his theory that whatever you tell yourself with positive conviction becomes a positive fact.

His most famous positive self-affirmation was – 'Every day, in every way, I am getting better and better.'

In 1843, Braid described hypnosis as a self-imposed trance-state brought about by auto-suggestion. Auto-suggestion is what you tell yourself and is the direct opposite to hetero-suggestion which is what *others* tell you about yourself. Someone may tell you you look unwell, and you will start to feel unwell, although you know you are, in fact, perfectly fit. To counter that negative hetero-suggestion, you tell yourself (auto-suggestion) that you are perfectly well. And you *will* feel well.

Exactly the same principle applies to all negative suggestions aimed at you from outside sources prompted by either unkind or well-meant suggestions. You may be told you will fail at an important interview, or will be unable to attain certain longed-for ambitions. You may have it suggested to you that past mistakes and failures will dog your present and future moves because what happened in the past is bound to happen again.

In 1884, Bernheim described self-hypnosis as a state of inside or outside suggestion. That is, today, the theory that is accepted by the British Medical Association, the Dental Association and by doctors, therapists and psychologists the world over.

The pain-negating powers of self-hypnosis help a person suffering from pain, often far more so than the taking of pain-killing drugs. Indian Fakirs walk on hot coals because they deny the existence of pain. The brain is sent messages that pain does not exist and, quite simply, to them it does not.

Mind over matter is the conquest of mental attitude over a given situation. Mind over mind is the triumph of the mind over the part of the mind that dismisses the problem which is proving troublesome. Self-hypnosis induces an automatic acceptability-state which receives the suggestions you make to yourself as positive, purposeful facts that have to be acted upon. They are unwritten memos to your mind.

Deeply-rooted negative impressions and memories of past failures, bereavements, fears and thoughts that haunt the subconscious mind can be brought to the surface of the conscious mind by self-hypnosis, analysed and finally dismissed so that the conscious mind is no longer over-shadowed and influenced by the mistakes and the misfortunes of yesterday.

It is the surprising but nevertheless very real function of self-hypnosis to bring negative memories and impressions to the surface and finally to show them as the true reasons for present, conscious failures, functional (of the mind) illnesses, obsessions, complexes, compulsions and phobias.

Curative self-hypnosis of this nature involves the subconscious recall of past negative actions prompted by the association of ideas developed by you. It is the revival of past experiences in relation to present hopes, ambitions and future moves.

Freud coined the word 'repressions' which means the removal of unpleasant or emotionally disturbing ideas from the conscious mind by the recall of subconscious facts and fancies that hamper present progress. Inhibitions, as well, respond to self-hypnotic suggestions that show them for meaningless and useless mental blocks that prevent freedom of thought and action. Inhibitions are usually emotional 'reasons' for not doing this, that or the other that come perfectly naturally to others.

In 1861, Maury used the term 'hypnagogic state' to describe the condition when one is about to fall asleep or is on the point of waking up. This state is excellent for inducing self-hypnotic suggestions of a positive nature that are 'slept on' and, upon waking, become realities.

Today's world is fraught with anxieties, but the power to resist negative influences lies with the individual who is ready and willing to practise self-hypnosis in the privacy of the home and the four walls of mind and imagination. This book will point the way.

Gilbert Oakley
London 1989

AUTHOR'S NOTE

All methods of inducing self-hypnosis described in this book have been tried and tested, as also have the auto-suggestive affirmations. All have been found to be effective, helpful and of extreme value to those wishing to improve their lives and to make additional progress in their domestic, commercial and social spheres.

The Glossary at the end of the book supplies additional information to those interested in the subject of self-hypnosis and relevant psychological studies that explain, in many ways, the phenomenon of hypnosis in general.

1

The Hypnotic Power of Your Personal Ego

If you are able to wake up each morning at a given time, without the aid of an alarm clock or, if you set the alarm but always wake up just before it goes off, you are an ideal person to practise self-hypnosis, for you are already hypnotising yourself to wake up in response to overnight commands you have made.

By determining to wake up at a certain hour you have placed your mind into an acceptivity state the night before and your subconscious mind takes over by informing your conscious mind when it is time to wake up.

If you can create that positive state of mind to control your sleeping and waking hours, then you can employ that mysterious element to see you safely and successfully through your conscious life. If, however, you have to rely on the alarm clock and would oversleep if it didn't go off, then you are not in a good acceptivity state to cause your subconscious mind to govern your conscious mind. However, the fact that you are reading this book establishes that you are already putting yourself into an acceptivity state to acknowledge the power of self-hypnosis.

At the commencement of your determination to master the art of self-hypnosis, and to condition your mind to obey the dictates of your subconscious mind, make every effort first to succeed in waking up when you have to, without the aid of an alarm clock.

This first step in self-hypnosis can be accomplished by laying your head upon your pillow before dropping off to sleep and telling yourself in an audible voice that you must wake up at the appointed time next morning. Name that time and see, in your mind's eye, the time registered on a clock. Let this seen-in-the-mind time be your final thought as you sink into sleep. Repeat this procedure for a few nights, while still setting the alarm as a precaution. After a few attempts, you will undoubtedly find that you *will* wake a few moments before the alarm is due to go off. After a while, there will be no need to set the alarm at all. The fact that you purposely do not set the alarm will further embed it into your subconscious that you just *must* wake up at the right time, for the alarm will no longer be there as a back-up. Once you have mastered this you are well on the way to being able to practise self-hypnosis in order to achieve success in far more important matters in life.

Consider, now, the power your personal Ego exerts upon you. The Ego is the 'I' of one's life; the part that makes you unique. Your Ego influences all you do in life, all you think about life and all you think about others with whom you come into contact. In all your waking hours you are influenced by your Ego. Hypnotised by it, in fact!

You are hypnotised by the fact that you are *you*. No-one else but you. You exist within the four walls of your imagination. You see the lives of everyone else through your own eyes. Although you may say glibly: 'I know how you must feel', you only know how another person feels by how you, yourself, would feel under certain given circumstances. You are limited by your own personal feelings and experiences.

Invariably, when a person tells you how they feel about such-and-such you at once tell them how *you*, in fact, feel about the same thing. Your Ego reaches out to cap or to match the other person's story. And, so very often, you hypnotise yourself into believing that you have had the same experience or feel just the same way. You are so influenced by what you do and think that it is not easy to get into the mind of another person. To compensate, you hypnotise yourself into thinking that you can.

In a wider sense you can hypnotise yourself into wishing for, and attaining, certain standards of living, certain career ambitions, certain relationships with others by the power of your Ego. When this influence is forceful enough you begin to realise those standards, ambitions, relationships, because you have, unconsciously, hypnotised yourself into achieving them. You have visualised and now you are able to realise.

This projection of the Ego is invaluable and is not to be misconstrued as egotism. We are dealing with the strong and silent projection of wishful thinking that, by the power of self-inducement on your part, is actually making these things happen. Because you desire them to happen, you visualise them as happening and now they are becoming a reality. This is a sound and sure way of using your personal Ego and does not annoy or antagonise others because it is confined within the secrecy of your personal thoughts and desires.

Positive self-analysis resulting in the realisation of your aims in life speaks of the inflated Ego. Defeat in ambitions illustrates the deflated Ego incapable of self-inducement towards success. Far too many people accept the deflation of their Ego and wallow in the masochistic 'pleasure' of it, enjoying, in a self-pitying way, the apparent uselessness of making any positive efforts to overcome it. They hypnotise themselves into accepting that all is hopeless, and in this state of mind give up trying.

If it is so very easy to hypnotise oneself into a negative frame of mind it becomes obvious that it must be equally easy to hypnotise oneself into a positive frame of mind. In the face of disaster you can shrug your shoulders, make the most of it. Or you can determine to rise above it. You can wallow in the sorrow of bereavement or find a new outlet that will help you to forget. It is all a matter of Egotistical (but very private and confined) self-hypnosis.

By the soothing influences of self-hypnosis, applied with absolute conviction that all will be right in the end, life can become livable, happiness realised, ambitions attained and functional ill-conditions cured for all time.

The imagination, spurred on by the Ego and gifted with the power to influence self to the point of dismissing the negative factors in life, can successfully change existence for the good if the positive urge to do so is there.

The adage that 'what will be, will be' is old-hat in the face of the new knowledge of what self-hypnosis can do for you. The positive phrases we must use are: 'What might be, won't be, if *I* don't want it to be!' and: 'What might be, will be, if *I* want it to be!'

Here are some negative Ego convictions that can be completely changed by positive self-hypnosis:

- **I am inferior.**
- **I am weak, fragile and prone to illness.**
- **I am an object of revulsion to others.**
- **I am useless.**
- **I might have a nervous breakdown.**
- **I cannot mix socially with others.**
- **I am suicidal.**

- I smoke too much.
- I drink too much.
- I would be ineffectual in a crisis; I would panic.
- I am self-conscious, easily embarrassed.
- The sight of blood terrifies me.
- I am victim to many phobias.

In succeeding chapters, self-hypnotic techniques will be given for overcoming these, and other, negative auto-suggestions.

Nature-Cure specialists say that as you eat, so you are. In the context of self-analysis, auto-suggestion and self-hypnosis it can be said without any doubt that 'What you *think*, so you *are*'.

2

Your Automatic
Hypnotic Reactions

Before we examine various methods of inducing self-hypnosis for the sake of eradicating the negative elements within ourselves, it will be interesting to see how we already take part in various acts of self-hypnosis without realising it!

In the case of an aching tooth, for instance, you will be advised to go to your dentist. You are rather afraid, possibly, of doing this and have, so far, resisted commonsense determinations to go to him.

On the morning of your visit, the tooth that raged yesterday is still being very painful. As you get ready to go the persistent aching seems to be diminishing somewhat. As your journey takes you nearer and nearer to the dental surgery, to your relief, the pain has now disappeared altogether!

But not, of course, because a small medical miracle has taken place.

Because your inherent and long-lived fear of the dentist has prompted your brain suddenly to deny the existence of toothache, therefore giving you ample excuse not to see the dentist after all. With some considerable measure of relief, you turn tail and go back home, much comforted and pain-free.

However, once in the safety of your home, the dreadful ache comes on again, probably with renewed fury!

The unconscious, self-hypnotic messages sent to your brain that the toothache no longer exists and therefore a visit to the dentist is unnecessary have performed their functions, so allaying your fears. But the bad tooth is still there, the nerve is still very much inflamed and you still need an extraction.

Your mind has told your body to build up resistance to the dentist and to the fact that you have an aching tooth. In so doing, your innate fear disappears, but not, of course, for very long.

You have hypnotised yourself into denying the existence of toothache through absolute fear. The inflamed nerve of the bad tooth has temporarily accepted this suggestion and has obeyed the commands of your mind-messages. But your self-induced trance-state soon breaks and you return to reality!

Fear, whether of pain, of failure, of competition, or one of the phobias later to be dealt with, is a self-induced hypnotic state which makes you hesitate to do something dangerous, to suffer discomfort, to make decisions or to do anything or to go anywhere that builds up feelings of apprehension within your mind.

Fear must not be confused with reasonable caution. Genuine fear is emotional behaviour based on the actions of the sympathetic nervous system that gives rise to trembling, prostration, paralysis of the thought-process resulting in immobility of physical action. Commonsense caution is a normal reflex thought or action dictated by knowledge of awkward or dangerous or questionable situations. Caution is normally overcome by reasonable analysis of a given situation and simple solutions arrived at to circumvent events that may cause anxiety.

Fear, on the other hand – as in phobias – is exaggerated beyond reasonable apprehension, and immediate solutions are not always quickly to hand. But self-induced reason can come to the rescue and self-hypnotic suggestions can put fear into focus.

Fear causes the brain to flash instant messages to halt forward progress of the body and mental action. It is an imagined 'road-block' built across the highway of action on command of the brain. Immediate action is either flight or fright, and in most cases, both. In bad cases, paralysis of the mind and body sets in and one becomes speechless, inactive, rooted to the spot.

The self-induced, self-hypnotic state caused by fear can make functional disability occur, in terms of imagined (but nevertheless very real) deafness, blindness, dumbness and, in the long run, amnesia in an attempt to shut out the memory of the particular fear.

These symptoms can equally arise in more simple sensations of fear, such as having to act in a play before an audience, deliver a lecture, attend an important job interview, settle an argument or dispute, confront an adversary, run in a competitive athletic event, make a vital decision affecting hopes and ambitions for the future or, indeed, something as simple as meeting someone for the first time.

All this illustrates how easily your mind can control your body in the *negative* things of life. How obvious must it be, therefore, to accept how well your mind can be made to control your body and your emotional reactions in regard to the *positive* things in life?

Your automatic hypnotic actions, induced by unconscious self-hypnosis, with which we are exclusively dealing in this chapter, must include the dreaded phobias, any one of which most certainly affects the average man or woman. Here are listed the most prevalent phobias, and, in the following chapter, they will be analysed and self-hypnotic suggestive therapy given for treatment and ultimate removal. Phobias are *exaggerated* fears and as such, can be whittled down to inconsequential confusions of thought that, upon examination, can be seen to be really quite foolish and totally unnecessary in the mature adult.

These phobias are considered to be exaggerated fears because they extend far beyond reasonable concern and a normal sense of precaution. They are invariably induced by *unconscious* self-hypnosis and, as we shall later see, can as easily be eradicated by *conscious* self-hypnosis.

Agoraphobia	Fear of Open Spaces
Claustrophobia	Fear of Enclosed Spaces
Nosophobia	Fear of Disease
Pathophobia	Fear of Suffering
Astraphobia	Fear of Thunder
Monophobia	Fear of Loneliness
Misophobia	Fear of Dirt and Germs
Acrophobia	Fear of Heights (*causing Vertigo*)
Hematophobia	Fear of Blood
Ochlophobia	Fear of Crowds
Erythrophobia	Fear of Blushing
Zoophobia	Fear of Animals
Xenophobia	Fear of Strangers/Foreigners
Insectophobia	Fear of Insects (*spiders, mostly*)
Nyctophobia	Fear of the Dark (*a childhood fear, mostly, in the adult*)
Aichmaphobia	Fear of Knives
Hamartophobia	Fear of Failure

Every irrational fear (or phobia) is a *state of mind* and every state of mind is a form of *self-hypnotic trance*, self-induced and *auto-suggested*.

When we have eventually dealt with the eradication of fear-thoughts by self-hypnosis, we will be able to turn our minds to the happier process of dealing with sleep-inducement, overcoming stammering, hesitation and procrastination, developing self-confidence, sowing the seeds of success, realising ambitions, being successful at interviews and the many, far more pleasant, aspects of happy living.

The auto-suggestive affirmations now to be considered in regard to overcoming phobias can be used without direct reference to the methods of self-hypnosis that will be explained in further chapters; but, *if* used under the influences of the self-hypnotic techniques to be explained later, they will, of course, prove to be even more effective. So bear your particular phobia in mind when learning the processes which will follow.

3

Auto-Suggestions for Defeating Phobias

Before we present positive affirmations for dealing with the negative influences of a particular phobia from which we may suffer, one thing must be made clear. On most bottles of medicine and packets of tablets bought across the counter there is usually the warning: 'If symptoms persist, see your doctor'. In this following survey of phobias and self-hypnotic suggestions for cures, let it be quite plain that, should phobic symptoms continue, or if phobic symptoms are very deeply-rooted, a doctor or psychiatrist should most certainly be consulted. Sometimes self-hypnosis is not sufficient for the removal of exaggerated fears when they persist. However, in the context of this book on self-hypnotism, it is to be taken for granted that all negative influences in the life of an individual seeking comfort from self-hypnosis are more or less on the surface and are, therefore, capable of cure by auto-suggestive therapy conducted by the individual.

Many, many phobias exist more in the imagination than in actual fact. Most of them arise through unpleasant childhood experiences which are recalled in adult life when similar situations occur, so creating phobias. An example is of a child being forced by its parents to sleep alone in a bedroom while a violent thunderstorm is raging. In later life, whenever a thunderstorm happens, the adult mind immediately goes back to the terrifying time in that bedroom, all alone, and the fear is relived all over again.

Again, in childhood, or in adolescence, you may have been bitten by a dog or fiercely scratched by a cat. Now you fear all dogs and cats, cannot bear to be near them, cannot stroke a cat or make a fuss of a dog. Both animals bring back, through association of ideas, the terrifying experience of former years.

As with the thunderstorm and the presence of those domestic pets, the relevant phobias set in.

Assuming, then, that your pet phobia is not too deeply-rooted or the result of so traumatic an experience that only psychiatric treatment will effect a cure, your personal efforts at self-hypnotic suggestions will most certainly help to eradicate it.

It is important first to discover by recall the basic reason for your particular phobia. This is known as abreaction – the re-acting of an unpleasant experience in order to discover and to accept its origin. A trained hypnotist will help you to recall by taking you into your past, under the influence of an hypnotic trance. You, however, in practising self-hypnosis, will take *your-self* back into your past and, by persistent soul-searching, dis-cover the true source of your emotional discomfort. We will call this process RECALL and the application of self-hypnotic sugges-tions we will call REPAIR.

Read the list of phobias in the preceding chapter again and decide the one, or the ones, from which you suffer. Apply the system of RECALL and REPAIR as suggested. RECALL means going back into your past (as far back as childhood if this is necessary) to remember the initial reason for your fear. Probe really deeply and with enthusiasm and determination until at last you remember what really happened that triggered off your present phobic obsession.

Then start to apply the self-hypnotic suggestions we call RE-PAIR, over and over again until you realise the futility of con-tinuing to give way to your irrational fear.

If it so happens that you only suffer from *one* phobia, discover what phobias your friends or members of your family are plagued by, and help them too, to apply these self-curative methods.

Fear of Open Spaces

RECALL Were you alone in a large field with a bull? Was there a high wind blowing? Were you accosted by a stran-ger? Had you strayed from your parents? Were you soaking wet from a downpour? Did you feel lonely and frightened? Were you lost? Did you become afraid to venture out into wide open spaces? Or were you out in crowds of people and became fearful in busy, traffic-filled streets? Did you lose your way? Did strangers harass you, or frighten you?

Let these sample questions awaken past thoughts in your subconscious until, suddenly, the truth dawns and you recall the very real circumstances that made you fearful of space, of crowds, of noise and confusion. Try really hard until at last you hit upon the beginnings of the matter. There is a very real reason why now, you are afraid to go out into the countryside or into wide open spaces or into crowded streets. Find out – now.

REPAIR   *Tell yourself*: What happened then will not happen again in the same way. I am no longer a child. I cannot get lost. Wide open spaces in the countryside are beautiful. The trees, the hedges, the lush green grass, the wide expanse of blue sky, all these things are beautiful. Alone in such lovely surroundings, I need know no fear. In crowded streets I am surrounded by many others, bent on their daily business as, indeed, I am on mine. Strangers will not accost me. I will no longer be afraid of those busy folk walking in front of me, behind me, by my side, going in and out of shops and buildings. They are not afraid of each other. They are not afraid of me. Why should I be afraid of them? I like the sounds of noisy traffic. All this is life being lived by busy people – and I am one of them.

The positive self-affirmations used in dealing with the phobias are of the most simple form. Later in this book you will learn methods of applying self-hypnotic suggestions by various means that will demand your full attention, and you will then be able to apply them to any phobic tendencies you may possess, with even more powerful force and satisfactory results than the simplified RECALL methods now being listed.

Fear of Enclosed Spaces

RECALL   Were you once shut up in a cupboard or other confined space by accident or by design? Perhaps you became locked in somewhere and could not get out? Maybe you were frightened when travelling on the Underground in a carriage packed with people and felt you were suffocating? Were you ever lost in a wood surrounded by tall trees and could not find your way out? Have you ever been trapped in

> a lift unable to attract attention and be released? Perhaps you were in a car that was travelling at high speed and were fearful there would be an accident.

Let those questions alert you to past negative experiences that made you feel closed-in, frightened, suffocating. Think really hard, way back into the past, to discover why you cannot bear to be in enclosed spaces now. There is a very real reason. Try to find it.

REPAIR *Tell yourself*: Those are all things of the past. I will never again be locked up in a dark cupboard. When I am travelling on the Underground I am surrounded by people who, though strangers to me, are friendly. They, too, feel hot and bothered, packed tightly as they are, but they are laughing and talking amongst themselves and are not afraid. Why should *I* feel afraid and imagine I am suffocating? There is plenty of air. If I am in a speeding car, to get out would be fatal and, anyway, I can open the windows and let the air in. The driver is friendly and knows what he is doing. Why not just sit back and enjoy the towns and the countryside? Soon the journey will be over and I will be able to step out again into God's good, clean fresh air! In a small space I am large, and in a large space I am small. But I am still myself. I must learn to work in a small office, live in a small room, for I am always larger than life all of the time.

Fear of Disease

> **RECALL** As a child, did you suffer from the usual childish complaints such as measles, chicken-pox and the rest? If you did, were you frightened by the general atmosphere of the 'sick room' and did you fear you would never ever escape from it? Did you, perhaps, suffer from a serious complaint that made visits to a doctor necessary but, to you, frightening? Were weeks spent in hospital surrounded, in your young mind, by all the bewildering aspects of doctors and nurses and painful treatments? Possibly you had to undergo an operation and were fearful of the trappings of an operating theatre, injections, the busy nurses, the stern-looking doctors, your tearful parents? Or did you come up

against young friends suffering from unpleasant illnesses or diseases and you shied away because you could not bear to look at them? Did you fear inoculations and examinations? Did your parents instil into you a horror of illness and disease? Did you have to see your mother or father dying from an incurable disease, or a friend or a relative? Did you ever think that you were suffering from a nasty disease, or imagine all sorts of pains? Did you feel you must have a bad heart, faulty respiration, or a variety of unpleasant health conditions? Did your parents tell you time and time again not to do this, touch that or take the other because it would make you ill? Have you grown up with a horror of doctors, nurses, hospitals, dentists?

REPAIR *Tell yourself*: I am fit and healthy and I thank God for that. I will not be a hypochondriac and imagine I have every illness under the sun! I will blot out from my mind all memories and impressions of childhood fears of illness and the memories of loved-ones afflicted with ills. I will not be a prey to reports of 'viruses' going round that everyone appears to be catching. I will revel in my good, God-given health and will not give way to a morbid fear of diseases which I am most unlikely to catch. I will not fantasise about high or low blood pressure. Neither will I fancy my heart is beating too quickly (or too slowly, come to that). And I will not imagine I have breathing difficulties and that slight rheumatic pains herald a heart attack or that a headache means a brain haemorrhage is coming on! I will not become a pest to my doctor, going to him with every imaginary complaint I suspect I am suffering from because I have read it in my Family Doctor book. I will not buy pills, potions and placebos to cure this, that and the other because I know that, after all, I am *not* suffering from anything at all.

But if you do have to visit your doctor with some genuine complaint, then you will do so without fear or apprehension because you know your doctor has the means to cure you and is certainly not a person to be feared.

RECALL In this context, 'suffering' includes emotional suffering as well as physical suffering.

Do you fear pain? Does that fear arise from a careless dentist who did not give you a powerful enough local anaesthetic? Have you suffered real pain from post-operative effects in childhood or in recent years? Have you endured pain as the result of an accident either in the past or recently? Let it be said that real pain is *real* pain. That is to say, Nature alone, together with properly prescribed pain-killing drugs, will eventually alleviate genuine pain arising from a real condition that exists as a result of an operation or an accident. Here we are dealing with psychosomatic, that is *imagined*, pain that can overwhelm us as compensation for worries and anxieties or as a subconscious excuse not to do a certain thing, start a certain job, confront a certain problem. This is 'escape' pain brought on by a very real desire *not* to do something we do not wish to do. The mind tells you that if you are ill and suffering from pain you will be excused from doing that which you find daunting. From those thinking-processes can be created the chronic headache, the migraine, the 'heart-pains', the breathing pains, the phantom ulcers, the hearing problems, the faintness, even the blackout. All escapism! Once the problem occasioning the psychosomatic disorder is removed, the 'pain' disappears. However, fear of suffering can be a very real thing and this very often prevents a genuine sufferer from asking the advice of a doctor, or facing up to an operation.

Fear of suffering can also be identified with a fear of disease and can be brought about by practically the same childhood or past experiences. So we will examine the other 'fear of suffering': the fear of having to endure poverty and want, unemployment, failure in everyday life or in one's love-life, fear of seeing others in pain, of witnessing accidents.

Did you, as a child or adolescent, have to see the physical suffering of loved-ones? Did you see a fatal street accident, experience poverty and want, fail, in early years at school or at a first job? Was a first love affair a disaster?

REPAIR   *Tell yourself*: I must cease to dwell on the sufferings of my loved-ones for now they are at peace. Early poverty in life is now being overcome by my present successes in life. I must not suffer fears of defeat and failure because, in early days, I experienced that. If my first love affairs were disastrous, I am now adult and mature and am able to handle such situations. If I cannot bear to look at serious street accidents, there is no reason why I should. If I cannot bear to see the suffering of others I will do no good by trying to soothe them. There are many people who are so sensitive to the emotional or physical sufferings of others that they can do no good to the sufferers. If I am one of those sensitive people, it is no crime on my part to turn away.

Fear of Thunder

RECALL   Were you, as a child, told that thunder was the Voice of God when he was angry, and that lightning was fire sent down from Heaven to set houses ablaze and to burn people! Were you left alone during thunderstorms and were you frightened out of your wits? Perhaps a friend or a relative was struck by lightning and suffered injuries or even death? Do you shiver and shake at the sound of thunderclaps and do you hide your eyes from flashes of lightning? Do you fear thunderstorms in the same way in which people feared air raids during the Second World War?

REPAIR   *Tell yourself*: Reasonable care taken during a thunderstorm, such as not standing under trees, not getting soaking wet but taking shelter, will protect you from attracting lightning. Dismiss old wives' tales of childhood about the Wrath of God and His Vengeance and all those mythological and illogical tales. Remember that nothing actually happened to you when you were forced to be alone during a thunderstorm. Try to think of thunder and lightning as a wonderful display of Nature at her most magnificent. Think of the infinite good lightning does to the green pastures, recharging them with life. Think of thunder as Nature's great symphony orchestra and learn, with interest and intelligence – to count the seconds between a flash of lightning and the sound of thunder so that you can calculate how far away the storm clouds are (5 seconds equals 1 mile). Learn to steady your nerves which may be upset by the noise of thunder. Stand by a window and force yourself to gaze up at the rushing, billowing, grey-black thunder clouds as they are blown along overhead, split in such magnificence by the vivid shafts of lightning. This is Nature at her best. Then smell the cool, sweet, fresh air after the storm has passed and listen to the birds in the trees as they start to sing again, knowing the storm has passed away.

Fear of Loneliness

RECALL Were you an only child? Or were your brothers and sisters loved more than you? Were you perhaps regarded as the proverbial 'black sheep' because you did not conform to convention, accept domesticity or the love of your parents? Did you seek your own company in preference to mixing with the rest of the family? At school, were you the butt of schoolmates' unpleasant jibes and jokes? Possibly you were bullied and made a scapegoat? Did you shy away from making friends, stay by yourself in the playground and refuse to take part in sport and games? Did teachers neglect and reject you and pass over you in preference to brighter, more communicative pupils? Do you now long to have friends, to enjoy a normal social life, to be well-liked at work? But, do you still isolate yourself as you did in earlier years, preferring your own company, fearing to mix with people in case you are rejected as you were in childhood and adolescence?

REPAIR *Tell yourself*: Brothers, sisters and even parents can sometimes be cruel and distant, unloving and uncaring. Schoolmates can also be cruel, vindictive, hurtful, bullying. But this is *now*, and I am an adult, surrounded by adults. They know nothing of my difficult upbringing, my unhappy schooldays, my self-sought solitude, my efforts to escape jibes and jeers. Do I have to live continually in the past? This is today and the people with whom I associate in everyday life are not those people of my past. They are eager to be friendly, interested in me and want me to be interested in them as well. I must stop fearing loneliness just because of what happened to me in the past. Probably there are others around me who are just as lonely. A word and a smile from me could make all the difference to them. I must determine, from today, to share my life and my thoughts and my feelings with others. I must start to mix socially, to join groups, dramatic societies, sports clubs, be more open and friendly with my colleagues at work. I must cease, from now on, being the introvert. Instead, I must try to be extrovert and forward-thinking. I must no longer wallow in the masochistic 'enjoyment' of loneliness, using it as an excuse to hide myself away from others. I'm just as acceptable to others as they could be to me, if only I will unwind and go out and seek their friendships and confidences. Nobody loves a loner. Anyhow, being a loner is to be selfish and self-centred, living only for oneself and doing nothing to make other people happy. Today, I will make it my job to make a friend – to make many friends, in fact!

Fear of Dirt and Germs

RECALL At home, when young, was your mother or father always forcing you to wash your hands, have too many unnecessary baths? Were you always being warned about the menace of dirt and germs? Did you have to listen to long diatribes about disease and infection caused by uncleanliness or untidiness about the home? Was personal hygiene almost a religion in your family?. Are you now, as an adult, obsessed by the thought of germs in your food and in your own home? Conditioned to an almost hourly ritual of washing your hands at home, at work and at play in order to escape the threat of multitudinous germs lurking round every corner, getting into your clothes, your fingernails, your hair? Are you worried when you go into a restaurant in case the cutlery and the tablecloths are germ-laden, cups dirty, food contaminated? Do you feel compelled to dust every seat upon which you sit, dread going to public lavatories for fear of what you might come into contact with? Do you have to run your finger along every ledge or table or window-sill to see how much dust is there? Do you dislike to shake hands with a stranger for fear of what might be transmitted to you?

REPAIR *Tell yourself*: As a mature adult, I now realise my mother (or father) was one of those people obsessed by the menace of dirt and germs, to an almost pathological degree. The bounds of decent, conventional clean-living were vastly exaggerated at home and this has been passed on to me in the same way that so many childhood obsessions, compulsions and complexes can be. They are frequently wished upon children by overanxious or misinformed parents. While observing the common decencies of personal cleanliness and hygiene, I will no longer permit it to be obsessive. I will forget and reject the paranoid attitudes of my parents and will, instead, lead a normal life, taking only those sensible precautions other people take. I will no longer be obsessed with the idea of having to wash my hands frequently, or of imagining there are germs in my food, in tableware and all around me. I will no longer have to test for dirt and dust in rooms and offices. I will be willing to shake hands with people to whom I am introduced without feeling I am likely to become contaminated. I will not, in other words, continue to be a crank about dirt and germs. There is no reason whatsoever why germs *should* be compelled to make a bee-line for me!

Fear of Heights

RECALL Was there a time, in your childhood or youth, when you looked down from a considerable height and felt absolutely dreadful? As if you were compelled to throw yourself down to the ground? Did you have to draw back quickly, as the world started to swim before your eyes and you felt you were losing your balance? Or, perhaps, on a holiday, you were climbing a hill and, looking down, those dreadful feelings of vertigo overcame you? If you had not been able to grab hold of a handrail or a tree, dizziness might well have caused you to plunge down. Even if you have never had such an unpleasant experience, you may still automatically have a fear of heights and be quite unable to attain them without having an attack of vertigo or, worse still, having that dangerous urge to throw yourself off the ledge or the hilltop.

REPAIR *Tell yourself*: This particular phobia is not merely a matter of the mind. It is a question of a sense of balance dictated to the brain by what the eyes see and by the messages sent to the brain and to the ears which are so connected with your sense of balance. You can, in search of a cure, force yourself to stand at the top of a high building, with the necessary precaution of a strong parapet to prevent you falling down. Or you can scale a hill or stand on top of a tower and force yourself to look down. Telling yourself you will not fall, you cannot fall, you do not want to throw yourself down may, after much repetition and effort, help you to overcome this fear. Sometimes, with this phobia the brain just will not accept commands of safety because the eyes and ears refuse to send confident messages to it that all is well. In this case it is unlikely that you will be able to overcome this fear very easily. Since scaling heights will not occupy much time in your everyday life, it is best to avoid heights; unless, of course, you are really determined to overcome this particular phobia. If, however, you have no choice, but find yourself at a considerable height, tell yourself that you cannot fall because there is an obstruction in front of you that will effectively prevent you from falling. Tell yourself you do not want to throw yourself off the edge. Walk away from the edge of whatever it is you are standing on and take deep, slow breaths until any attack of vertigo clears away, your head ceases to pound and your breathing becomes normal again. Of all the phobias, fear of heights is the least bothersome, since one does not necessarily have to invite it.

Fear of Blood

RECALL Was your very first sight of blood that of your own or of somebody else's? How did you react at the sight of your own blood? Did it happen because of an accident or injury or through having a medical blood-test? Did it make you feel faint, even cause you to pass out in childhood or in young adulthood? If it was the sight of someone else's blood because of an accident or injury, a car crash, a fall or an act of violence, did it make you shudder? Did you have to turn away from the sight? Were you sick? Did you find the sight of blood repulsive? If you witnessed an accident involving a cat or dog or other animal, did that cause you similar discomfort? Do you now fear cutting or even scratching your flesh in case you draw blood? Even if a loved-one has an accident which causes a flow of blood, are you so badly affected that you have to turn away and are unable to give assistance to prevent a serious loss of blood in the victim? Would you shudder away from having a blood transfusion in a hospital? Would you be unable to give blood as a donor?

REPAIR *Tell yourself*: Blood is my life force. It is the life force of every living human being, of every single animal. I mostly fear the sight of it because it is *red*. Red is the colour of anger, passion, war and conflict. I am fortunate to have good, healthy blood in me. I am lucky not to be anaemic as so many others are. Red is also the colour of *love*. It is pure and wholesome, it is life itself. Without blood I would not be alive and fit and healthy. Without blood those whom I love and live with would be dead. I should not turn away from the sight of blood being shed as the result of an accident. I must and *can* steel my nerves against nausea if it means I can help and bring assistance to a person suffering from blood-loss. If some time I have to have a blood transfusion I must not fear it but must welcome it, for some donor, somewhere, is making it possible for me to recover from my illness and to become strong again. If I am required to give blood in an emergency I must feel happy that I am being given a chance to help someone else, to give someone else a chance to go on living. If I see an animal in distress and losing blood, I must also do all I can to help and not turn away in weakness or in disgust. If I injure myself and bleed I must not faint at the sight of my own blood but I must take all reasonable steps to stem the flow without being squeamish.

The remaining eight phobias should be dealt with in a similar manner, firstly *Recalling* past memories, impressions and experiences which have led to the present phobic compulsion and, secondly, *Repairing* the damage of the past by making positive auto-suggestive affirmations as shown for the first nine phobias, in order to rid yourself of the unpleasant symptoms created by the past.

The eight remaining phobias with which you should deal following the lines already shown are:

Fear of crowds
Fear of blushing
Fear of animals
Fear of insects
Fear of the dark
Fear of knives
Fear of failure
Fear of strangers/foreigners

As already stated, the auto-suggestive affirmations in dealing with phobias can be used without actual self-hypnotic procedures but, if used in the ways to be described, the results will naturally be far more satisfactory and lasting.

4

Getting Started with Self-Hypnosis

When a hypnotist places a subject in an hypnotic trance, the subject can hear all the commands given to him by the hypnotist, but he hears them and receives them into his subconscious mind and reacts to them upon being awakened from the trance when his conscious mind takes over again.

When you place yourself into a self-hypnotic trance, you know what positive affirmations you are giving to yourself and you can also hear yourself commanding this that and the other. But the affirmations are being absorbed by your subconscious mind, and, upon taking yourself out of your self-induced state of hypnosis, your conscious mind takes over again and acts upon those positive auto-suggestions.

Your self-induced trance state is not a blackout by any means. It is a technique of blotting out all circumstances and surroundings and thoughts other than the dominant thoughts of that moment, the thoughts of what is perplexing you and what you wish to remove from your mind.

The very fact that you know something is not right is a state of mind brought on by self-hypnosis in your *conscious* state. That is in direct contradiction to a self-induced state of mind that tells you all *is* well. Many negative states of mind over persons, places and things do not actually exist outside the four walls of your imagination. Other people are not aware of them, for they are locked up in the dark recesses of your mind.

Fears, complexes, compulsions, repressions or inhibitions are known as hypnoidal objects, those emotions, in fact, that trigger off your negative states of mind. When you are confronted by the object (or atmosphere) of your fear, you at once hypnotise yourself into an acceptivity state of mind to acknowledge that particular fear. Equally, you can hypnotise yourself into *rejecting* that particular fear. It is a question of logic. If your mind can accept a negative thought, it is also able to accept a positive thought which automatically can destroy the negative thought.

Fearing a meeting with someone, or an important interview, or a hazardous journey, or a visit to someone who is ill, you can hypnotise yourself into manufacturing a negative state of mind. By the time the dreaded situation takes place defeat stares you in the face because *you have told yourself* it will be so.

Self-hypnosis prepares the mind to receive positive suggestions that will sink deep down into the subconscious mind and thereafter control conscious actions to the good. Usually, only a state of light self-hypnosis is attained by self-application, but this is quite enough to make the therapy very workable and helpful.

Bear in mind that no system of self-hypnosis will succeed the *very first time*. It is a question of repetition, practising your chosen method time and time again until at last you really start to find it is finally working.

In chapter one we listed some negative Ego convictions that you may well be suffering from. They were . . .

- **I am inferior.**
- **I am weak and fragile and prone to illness.**
- **I am useless.**
- **I cannot mix socially with others.**
- **I might have a nervous breakdown.**

You may suffer from one, two or *all* of these negative convictions. They all have a bearing on each other, the final conviction being that you might have a nervous breakdown.

Now – try *this*.

Sit back in a comfortable armchair in your room, with a powerful bright light placed on a low table right in front of you. Angle the lamp so that you can stare directly at the light bulb. The room must be entirely darkened so that everything is shut out from your gaze apart from the vivid white light. If you wear glasses, do not remove them. Let your arms rest easily on the arms of your chair and relax yourself slowly, from the feet upwards, until you really feel quite limp. Stare unflinchingly at the bright white light for several moments. Shut out all existing thoughts except the one dominant one of that negative conviction you want to banish for ever. For a short while, literally wallow in the thought of your supposed failing. (I am inferior or weak and fragile and prone to illness and I am useless in all things and to others, or I cannot mix with people or I fear a nervous break-down.)

Very soon you will find the bright white light seems to be moving towards you and retreating from you at intervals and starts to be surrounded by an aura, a halo, much likened to the colours of the spectrum. Soon you will find your eyelids are drooping and you feel sleepy.

As soon as that begins to happen start repeating in a loud, commanding tone of voice applicable auto-suggestions that have a direct and positive bearing on the particular state of mind you wish to eradicate. For instance,

- *I am not inferior, I am as good as anyone else. I am subject to no one.*
- *I am as good as the next person. I am capable and I am a positive person.*
- *I am strong. I am not weak. I will not be ill. There is no reason why I should be ill. I am not fragile but I am in good health.*
- *I am far from useless. I have my own special abilities and capabilities. I can be useful to others.*
- *People will like me socially. I must start to mix more, go out and about. I must stop being a recluse. I must be outgoing.*
- *I will not have a nervous breakdown. There is no reason why I should have a nervous breakdown. A nervous breakdown is a sign of emotional weakness. I am not weak, but emotionally strong.*

Repeat these positive affirmations over and over again as the bright white light burns into you! When you start to feel exhausted and really sleepy, allow yourself to fall into a light sleep, conscious, all the time, of the light still on.

After a while, whether you have been asleep or just relaxing in a pleasant manner, get up from your chair, illuminate the room again, switch off the bright light. The session is at an end.

After you have carried out this technique of inducing a self-hypnotic trance several times (daily or nightly, if possible) you will find your conscious mind is beginning to bring to the surface the subconscious affirmations you have sown into it during those sessions. It is of the utmost importance from then on, to start to *act* upon them. To turn them into actual facts.

Very soon you will begin to have more confidence, to feel physically stronger; to dismiss foolish thoughts and fears of illness; to start to make the most of your capabilities and abilities that possibly you have so far denied you possess.

You will find yourself going out more, to pubs or clubs or dances. Mixing more with people at your place of work. Going out a few evenings a week rather than sitting staring at television all of the time. Nervous breakdown? Perish the thought! That's not for *me*!

The keyword is *persistence*. The intention is positive and progressive, all of the time, during all hypnotic suggestive-therapy described so far and later, in this book. It is by no means a one-off thing. It is all a question of perseverance all of the time, more especially in the face of initial disappointments and delays in progress. The mind, convinced of negative things must have time to switch over to positive thoughts and things. Your subconscious mind is tricky and has to be manipulated with care and consideration!

Before you drop off to sleep every night, and while using this particular method of inducing self-hypnosis, repeat the positive affirmations just listed that have particular emphasis on your state of mind. Upon waking in the mornings, you will have sown those thought-seeds even deeper into your subconscious in order to resurrect them in your conscious mind during the day.

5

The Counting Method

The self-induced hypnotic trance-state is as natural as is normal sleep itself. The implantation of positive suggestions into the subconscious during a self-hypnotic trance-state is as natural as telling a sleeping person that all will be well upon awakening.

Natural sleep is the condition when nature gives the conscious mind a period of rest and allows the subconscious to take over. It is then that dreams occur which, upon awakening, can very often not be recalled in their entirety because they are, by then, buried deep within the subconscious. However, with the considerably lighter 'sleep' of self-hypnosis, the suggestions (dreams) put into the subconcious do not go so very deeply. Consequently, they are more easily recalled, and acted upon, in the conscious state.

Provided no negative fears have been set up in your mind by outside opinions or negative attitudes towards the value of self-hypnosis, and if no suggestions of 'evil', Black Magic or harmful results have been suggested by sceptics, self-hypnosis can be induced, with no harmful effects and most certainly with every hope of eradicating functional ills, the alleviation of mild pains and the eradication of compulsions, complexes and inhibitions.

Auto-suggestion can very often be by accident, whereas self-hypnotic suggestion is by deliberate design. An example is of a man driving a car and seeing a serious accident involving a car in the street. This sudden assault on his mind unnerves him and he suggests to himself that he cannot continue to drive his own car on that particular journey in case the same fate overtakes *him*. But, were he to take a rest from driving, it would be possible to defy the negative auto-suggestion, by replacing it with a designed, positive self-hypnotic suggestion that he could, in fact, continue to drive in spite of the accident he has witnessed.

The well-adjusted, balanced man or woman keeps a positive picture of success in the forefront of his or her mind all of the time. The most simple of compliments offered by another person often works wonders: 'You *are* looking well!' (You preen yourself and, yes, you actually *do* look well.) 'You *are* clever! (And you begin to believe it.)

In the absence of such outside compliments you can, of course, so boost yourself that you begin to look good, and fit and well, to onlookers.

Go to sleep worried and the odds are you will wake up worried. Go to sleep happy and you will wake up happy. Which brings us to a second method of inducing self-hypnosis. This depends upon the subtle effects of sleep and its power to help you to wake in the morning, independent of outside negative suggestions, and arms you with auto-suggestive positive affirmations that you deliberately design to implant into your subconscious during the hours of sleep.

The Counting Method

This is self-induced hypnosis by counting before going to sleep.

Relax, in bed, by yourself, in a dark room.

Let your body grow limp from the feet upwards, willing yourself to be completely mentally and physically relaxed.

When you are sure you *are* completely relaxed and detached, begin to count slowly up to ten, with your eyes wide open in the darkness.

Then count again, slowly, up to nine. Count again, from one to eight and so on through one to seven, to six, to five, to four, to three, to two, to one.

Repeat this routine of count-down over and over until you begin to feel nice and drowsy.

Saving yourself, in time, from dropping off to sleep, say to yourself, in a loud voice: 'When I start to count again, down to one, I will, by the time I reach one be in an hypnotic sleep-state. I will then have sent positive suggestions direct to my subconscious mind'.

Now, start counting, but, this time, silently, to yourself. Between each number you count in your mind, give yourself positive affirmations either spoken or in your mind, such as:

- *When I wake up tomorrow I will feel very happy and content.*
- *Tomorrow I will no longer feel worried.*

- *I will feel better than ever in health, tomorrow.*
- *I will find all my problems easier to solve when I wake up.*
- *Tomorrow, I will be calm, cool and decisive.*

Use all or some of these affirmations or formulate your own to suit your unique requirements. Get in as many positive suggestions relevant to your particular wishes between each *mental* count up to ten.

If you have not fallen off to sleep by number six or seven, continue the count up to ten and, as long as you can keep awake, start the mind-count again, slipping in the positive affirmations in between each number as before, until finally you do go to sleep.

When you awaken next morning, if you have been positive enough and have had complete faith in your auto-suggestions, and have been convinced they will work on you for the good that very day, *they will*.

If, however, they do not appear to be very effective that first time, try the same routine the following night in bed, for a week or so. Finally, you will, without doubt, discover the auto-suggestive therapy is beginning to have a good effect on you, for the subconscious mind cannot be fooled and does not readily dismiss things it is told to absorb and to act upon.

After a short time of practising this method, your subconscious mind will have absorbed and be able to recall the positive suggestions you have put into it. This is a law of human nature that is almost impossible to defeat, otherwise we would not be in possession of *two* minds: the conscious and the subconscious.

If, by any chance, you find it difficult to drop off to sleep in the ordinary run of events and you are not giving yourself auto-suggestive therapy on the lines described, but just wish to be able to go to sleep on command, use the following technique.

Relax easily as already described, in bed, in the dark. Tell yourself silently that, at the count of thirty, you will go to sleep. Start to count, in your mind, with your eyes closed and your body completely relaxed from one to thirty, slowly and in measured silent tones. If it does not work at first, start the count again. If you are still unsuccessful in inducing sleep quickly, do the same thing the following night. Very soon you will find your subconscious mind retaining and accepting the idea that by the time you reach the count of thirty you *will* drop off to sleep.

Perseverance, persistence and a positive conviction that you are succeeding in inducing self-hypnosis is essential, with all methods in this book, if they are to be totally successful. Even if you have to practise one or all of the techniques in this book for a month or so, do not give up for, eventually, your subconscious mind will become irrevocably reconciled to the stream of suggestions you are putting into it and it *will* start to obey.

In the next chapter, we will examine a further method of self-hypnosis called the Close-up Method.

6

The Close-Up Method

The point right between the eyes, where the pituitary gland is situated, and the nape of the neck, are two very vulnerable parts of the body. If an athlete stares at the nape of the neck of a runner whom he wishes to overtake in a race very soon he will find he *is* able to overtake him. Or, if someone stares hard at the back of *your* neck, the odds are that, after a while, you will feel compelled to turn round. This is one of the mysteries of human nature; unexplained, possibly, but very real, nevertheless.

In addition, if you stare at a person right between his eyes while trying to put over an important point, you will find you are able to exert an influence over him that would not be so easily achieved if you were looking at any other part of his face.

Equally, if you stare very closely at a small object held near to your eyes, you will feel a certain drowsiness coming over you the longer you hold your attention focused on the object. Quite soon, you will be conscious also of the fact that the peripheral views from both your eyes become misty. Eventually, the objects and the spaces right and left of your eyes will become invisible to you. What you will then be fully concentrating your gaze upon will be the small object set very close to your eyes and, most importantly, lined up with the vital spot *between* your eyes. This self-hypnotic method is called the *Close-up Method* and is exactly similar to a hypnotist's instructions to a subject to concentrate steadily on a small bright object held very close to the subject's eyes. The difference is, of course, that you are not a hypnotist's subject, but *your own* subject, when using this particular method and all other self-hypnotic techniques explained in this book.

When you have decided to try the Close-up Method, find a small square of stiff white cardboard. With a compass draw a number of decreasing circles, one inside the other, on the white cardboard in as black a pen or pencil as possible. The widest, outside circle should be about eight inches in diameter and each circle drawn by the compass reducing down to about a quarter of an inch. In the centre of the final circle, draw a very heavy black dot that focuses attention upon the very centre of the circles.

Now stretch yourself comfortably on your bed, lying on your stomach and prop the square of white cardboard up against the headboard, on a pillow, very, very close to your eyes. With your hands clasped together resting just above your chest and your elbows at right angles to your body, relax, as before, from your toes upwards to your head, willing yourself to grow comfortably limp and relaxed.

When you are satisfied that, in fact, you *are* completely relaxed, and that your arms are free from pressure underneath your chest and your hands are loosely clasped together, begin to stare hard at the black circles on the white board that now must be about six inches or so from your face.

After a few moments, you will find that the clear lines of the reducing circles seem to be converging one into the other. Very soon after that, the black dot in the centre of the circle will appear to you to be growing larger and blacker. At the same time, you will discover that the vague impressions of objects seen out of the corners of your eyes are dissolving into nothingness and that all you can now see are the misty black circles melting into each other and the dominant black spot in the centre of the card.

You have now narrowed down your vision and concentrated your thoughts upon the one object, the black spot, surrounded by misty, indeterminate circles. You have also narrowed down your thinking capacity so that it is taking in one vision and one thought to the exclusion of all others: the black spot and the *thought* of that black focal point.

Still totally relaxed, for you have taken away all thoughts about your body for the time being, you can begin to recite the auto-suggestive affirmations necessary to tackle the problem in hand.

This synchronisation of visual and mental 'one-ness' now enables you to cut yourself off from outside influences for the duration of this session.

Your eyes and your mind are, together, narrowed down to a thin but vital and penetrating beam of thought which must now be occupied with the self-hypnotic suggestions you are going to give yourself.

Say to yourself now, in a low voice:

- *'My eyes are beginning to grow heavy. I cannot hold my eyelids open.*
- *I am going to sleep but, while I am asleep, I will be able to hear myself saying how I want to feel when I wake up.'*

Repeat that several times until you discover that you are not asleep really, but in a self-induced hypnotic trance similar to that achieved by a trained hypnotist. There will be no resistance on your part as there might well be if a hypnotist was attempting to put you into a trance, for it is entirely *your* will and *your* desire to be in a temporary trance-state and you are totally in command of the situation. Now begin to give the commands to your subconscious mind; for example:

- *'My bad headache will go. My rheumatic pain will go.'*
- *'That worrying problem will sort itself out.'*
- *'I will see things far more clearly now.'*

and so on, according to your current worry or problem.

Persist with your positive affirmations which, although you are by now in a light self-hypnotic state, you will be conscious of and can actually hear yourself repeating. If, by any chance, you do drop off to sleep, all well and good, for, when you wake up you will find that your auto-suggestive dictates will have sunk even deeper into your subconscious and you will be even more receptive to the suggestions of your conscious mind. Succumbing to real sleep in these or in any self-hypnotic situations is not failure, but success! Happily, not going completely to sleep is equally effective.

When this particular session is over and you either awaken from a genuine sleep or decide to conclude the therapy, get up from the bed, reflect upon the positive thoughts you have been feeding into your mind just as one feeds information into a computer, and relax. Looking at it logically, the human brain is, without a doubt, the original computer, to be controlled by the human touch, supplying a reliable print-out.

Again, it is stressed that this routine, like the first described, and like the other methods later in the book, may not yield positive results right away. Perseverance is vitally necessary all along the line. Never allow any doubts to creep in, in the light of initial failures. You are totally in command of your own mind and no one should make you doubt it.

You will find that the actual fact of settling down to enjoy a self-hypnotic session will induce an immediate state of expectation which will put you in the right frame of mind to accept the positive suggestions.

Always tell yourself, and firmly believe it, that the suggestions you are putting into your mind *will* work at a date specified by you. This is known as post-self-hypnotic suggestion. Often a trained hypnotist will put post-hypnotic suggestions into the mind of a subject to take effect at a later date in the same way.

You will tell yourself that your positive suggestions will take effect at the time that you have commanded them to be effective whether it be at an interview or other future important occasions.

After coming out of a self-hypnotic session, do not start to worry all over again about the anxieties, the problems or the pains that you have been seeking to change or alleviate. Consider them to be over and done with from the moment of ceasing the session, and happily anticipate the gradual disappearance of any pain you have sought to be rid of. The assured, determined and accepted positive state of mind simply must be maintained, allowing no negative thoughts to creep in and to spoil it all. Believe and it will, indeed, be so!

7

Five Fundamental Facts

Before disclosing and describing further methods of inducing self-hypnotic states, here are five facts about the process it will be beneficial to learn.

1 Hypnosis inducing an hypnotic trance illustrates a mind that is in a high state of suggestibility and acceptivity.

2 You have to create, within your mind, this state of suggestibility and acceptivity by having absolute faith in the power of the suggestions you make and the genuine and wished-for *acceptance* of these suggestions.

3 The particular methods of self-hypnosis you choose as being the best for you to employ in your search for self-help must capture your imagination and fire your enthusiasm and you must be convinced they are the *best* methods for you.

4 You must believe, absolutely and entirely, in your power over your own mind and the power of your subconscious to dictate to your conscious mind exactly and precisely what you want it to do.

5 You should understand that you must be sufficiently conscious to be able to give yourself positive suggestions, but sufficiently under your 'own influence' to be able to absorb them into your subconscious. However, genuine, deep sleep after a self-hypnotic session is not a bad thing as it gives your subconscious even more time to absorb your commands and ultimately to act on them.

Those who believe in the power of prayer find it is very often a powerful form of self-hypnosis, bringing about calm, peace of mind, serenity, hope for the future. The words of prayers, the words and the melodies of hymns, are verbal and audible positive affirmations for help and succour. The priestly tone of the preacher in the pulpit is, itself, a voice apart that induces hope, alleviates fears and brings calm to a congregation that is, unwittingly, being led into a state of self-hypnosis.

On the more violent and material side, crashes, bangs, explosions, the sound of shattering glass, shouts and screams, bring about an immediate reaction for self-protection and preservation. The crackle of flames, the sound of sirens, the shouts of crowds, arouse the instincts, by sudden self-hypnotic suggestions, to have thoughts of flight, fright or fear. Subconscious memories and impressions of danger, fear or anger surge up into our conscious minds and prompt us into immediate action by suddenly induced self-hypnosis. We then act as we have been conditioned to act in the past either bravely, or in a cowardly manner. We may faint to avoid the alarming conditions or we may take positive action to help. We self-hypnotise ourselves into being positive or negative.

From the moment we are born, and accepting we are normal, mentally and physically, we live a life balanced between the subconscious and the conscious minds. Between what happened in the past (in childhood, adolescence) and what is happening, now, in the present. And the future is in many ways determined by positive or negative influences retained by the subconscious and allowed to dominate and to control the conscious mind.

Self-hypnosis helps us to control the negative suggestions put to us by the subconscious mind relating to negative experiences of the past. Schoolday traumas create the bully or the hooligan or the timid loner. Even before that, parental and domestic influences make for positive or negative attitudes that are reflected later in life because of what we remember and see fit to apply to adulthood, for better or for worse. First sexual experiences very often make or mar the adult sex-life, dictate the love scene, marriage harmony, influence hetero-sexuality and, in some instances, induce homosexuality, lesbianism or asexuality, even perversion.

What happened in the past influences the present and often shapes the future.

But, when we know things are going wrong, getting out of proportion, growing menacing and harmful, and becoming detrimental to progress, then comes the time to attempt to readjust and apply new concepts of living. Self-hypnosis helps that to happen if we are ready and willing to change our ways and are intelligent enough to recognise where we are going wrong and what past influences are making us go wrong.

When you sincerely welcome an examination of conscience through self-hypnosis properly conducted, life can be put into focus again.

Now we will examine a third way of inducing self-hypnosis towards creating that better self.

8

The Audio Method

The Audio Method of inducing a state of self-hypnosis embraces the technique of focusing thought into one channel by employing the use and the influence of sound. Music lovers can conjure up vistas of rolling seas, magnificent thunderstorms, the peace and the quiet of a country scene or the bustle of city life, by the musical pictures painted by the composer.

The sighing sound of the wind in the trees, whistling and whining round the rooftops, the pattering of raindrops on window panes, the gentle sound of birds roosting at twilight; these vital and dramatic assaults upon the ear have the power to calm inflamed nerves, dissipate destructive thoughts and doubts, curb a rising temper or arouse the emotions of sentiment.

On every such occasion, an unconscious and an unacknowledged self-hypnotic trance is induced during which, temporarily, the conscious mind gives way to subconscious memories and impressions associated with the particular musical sounds being heard.

When a deliberate attempt is made to use the powerful influence of music to lull the mind into a trance state and sow positive auto-suggestions into the subconscious, this can be found to be a very useful technique in inducing self-hypnosis.

Begin with the mechanical sound and the visual movement of a metronome, the tempo-timer used by musicians.

The metronome, when set off, sends an inverted pendulum moving backwards and forwards, in a measured and pre-set motion. At the same time a constant and monotonous 'click - click' is heard as the pendulum reaches its right- and left-hand limits. Here is the perfect instrument to provide a regular, insistent motion while, at the same time, emitting a persistent sound. The eyes are captured and riveted, the ears are gently assaulted by the sound.

Assuming you have been able to buy or borrow a metronome,

place it on a table about two feet away from the chair on which you are sitting, so that your eyes are on a level with the swinging pendulum.

Start the metronome working and sit, with your arms folded on the table top and your gaze fixed on the swinging arm. Follow, with your eyes, the rhythmic left-to-right motion while, at the same time, allowing your ears to receive and your mind to register the monotonous clicking sound.

Quite soon you will find that the sound dominates all other sounds that may be coming to your ears, both from the street outside and from other parts of the building. At the same time, you will realise that all peripheral sights are no longer within the range of your gaze and that the only thing your eyes are now registering is the persistent swing of the pendulum. Next, you will discover that this sight and this sound begin to weigh on your thinking-processes and that your eye-muscles are growing heavy and tired. This will make itself evident after about five minutes.

Now it is time to begin to give yourself the auto-suggestive affirmations you have decided upon before the session started. Speak to yourself softly, your voice not rising above the sound of the clicking pendulum. Space out your words so that the syllables synchronise with the movement and sound of the metronome.

It is advisable to memorise your affirmations rather than have them written down, for you should not take your eyes away from the pendulum until you have finished.

It is important that, not only should you synchronise your words and syllables with the sounds of the pendulum, but your eyes, also, should move in sync with its movements.

Repeat the affirmations over and over again until, possibly, you find you cannot stand the visual and audible strain any longer. When that happens, you must stop the metronome and take a short rest or light sleep on your bed. This gives time and opportunity for the auto-suggestive affirmations and commands to sink deep down into your subconscious.

You should carry out this process a few more times, repeating the same suggestions and taking a short rest in between.

As with the other methods so far described, they should be repeated time and time again until you feel they are having an effect. You can either keep to the techniques that work best for you, or you can vary things by using different techniques alternately. You will soon discover which suits you best or whether *all* methods are having positive results, in which case you can choose whichever technique your mood dictates.

With all these methods of inducing self-hypnosis you will soon find that, upon settling yourself down to any particular session, you will automatically hypnotise yourself into a state of acceptability because that has proved to be the situation in previous experiments. It is essential to plan ahead before you start any particular session. Do not go into the thing haphazardly. Plan the auto-suggestive affirmations you wish to give yourself before starting, whether they are to deal with your health, with stopping smoking, cutting down drinking, overcoming inferiority, blushing, or ridding yourself of a phobia. A different plan can be made for each session. It is not advisable to attempt to cram positive suggestions on a variety of problems into one session. Select just two or three each time, for one hundred per cent success.

As a trained hypnotist always predetermines what suggestions he is going to put into the mind of a subject, so you must know exactly what suggestions you are going to put into your own mind at any given session.

As far as using music is concerned your choice will depend on what works best for you. It is possibly difficult for some people to believe that loud pop music or heavy-metal could bring about an acceptivity state for self-hypnosis. But it does have a hypnotic, insistent beat which could work well for those who enjoy listening to it.

Others may find that certain 'classical' pieces immediately calm or rouse their emotions to the right self-hypnotic state for accepting whatever positive suggestions they want to implant in the sub-conscious.

Your choice of music will be made in the light of the particular hypnotic state you wish to induce and that will be determined by the auto-suggestion you intend to implant in your sub-conscious. For instance, the 1812 Overture would well suit the individual who wishes to inspire himself to do courageous things and to forge ahead in life. Ballet music, say from Swan Lake, would be suitable for the person in love who wishes to make himself or herself more assertive, demonstrative and attractive to his or her lover. Humorous, light music from Gilbert and Sullivan would suit the individual trying, by auto-suggestive therapy to cultivate a sense of humour and to enjoy a better social life. The calming influence of chamber music should suit the person telling himself to feel better after an illness. A Strauss waltz or two could inspire the would-be socialite to improve his personality and to make the grade in his social life. There would be no harsh sounds, merely the soft and lilting three-four measure that speaks of perfect rhythm and bodily and emotional control.

Having assured yourself of your personal musical taste, go to bed with the soft or exciting sounds of one of your favourite pieces playing in the bedroom where you are, preferably, alone. Repeat the chosen positive affirmations decided upon in advance as your head rests comfortably on the pillow and you are listening to the music that suits your present mood. Repeat the affirmations over and over again until either the music comes to an end or you drop off to sleep. If you are not yet ready to fall off to sleep start the music up all over again. Try to repeat this procedure night after night, until you are satisfied your subconscious is receiving the messages you are giving to it. You can obtain special tapes for inducing hypnotic trances, but it would be better to make your own, then you can tailor them to your own very individual requirements.

In the next chapter we will consider negative ideas and inhibitions and complexes that an individual can develop through past, unfortunate experiences but which can, upon being revealed, be eradicated from the subconscious by laying them bare and refusing to permit them to influence the present.

9

Cure Your Negative Ideas and Inhibitions

Misguided thoughts and ideas can produce stomach ulcers, boils, hysteria, euphoria or elation.

Such negative impulses in the mind can create hypochondria, worry, nervous debility, depression and a host of other anxiety states.

Such negative impulses and ideas can be pumped into the mind by unwitting and unconscious self-hypnosis brought about either by negative suggestions from others, by alarming sights seen, or by our own alarmist and fearful thoughts. The saving grace can be positive thoughts of self-assurance brought on by ourselves, to counter and defeat the negative influences.

The mind is always ready to react to crisis. Only too readily, with some people, for they condition themselves to accept crisis, trouble, drama, disappointment and failures. The mind is a sensitively tuned 'radio' station, ready to receive signals, good or bad, from all sides. The self-hypnotiser should adjust his wavelengths to accept signals of his own choice and preference and to 'jam' all incoming signals that he wants to reject.

Self-hypnosis involves the control of reflexes to which our minds and our bodies are automatically tuned. These are called conditioned reflexes and are, in fact, our reactions to various happenings, shocks, fright, fears, joys, happinesses and good news. Folk react in many different ways according to the dictates of their conditioned reflexes. There is the *flight-fright-fear* reflex in times of danger. The *fight-it-now* reflex. The *faint-on-sight* reflex. The *hypochrondriacal* reflex that convinces illness is present or the mind is becoming confused. The *failure* reflex that accepts defeat without question and with resignation. The *euphoria* reflex that raises joy to an unbalanced and unrealistic height, out of all proportion to actual facts.

Your conditioned reflexes are governed by experience and knowledge of things seen, sounds heard, scents smelled, sensations felt. Your reflex action to a scent may be a pleasant memory of a past love. Or a pleasant cooking smell tickles your palate. Music brings to mind a dramatic, pleasant or even unhappy event of the past. The feeling of textures brings to mind the clothes of a friend or the curtains and carpets of a home no longer playing a part in your life. These reflex-conditioned memories and associations may have just a passing effect on you, or they may spur you on to find a lost love, revisit an old home or relive a pleasant experience.

Certain failures in the past may condition you to reject attempts now to try again, because the influence of past failure convinces you that you will once again fail. Pain, experienced in the past, might well prevent you seeking medical help for fear of having to suffer the same pain again. Fear of a dentist is a fine example of this, as already explained.

With self-hypnosis you can change a negative, reflex, conditioned action by understanding and accepting the influences of past, self-imposed, self-hypnotised fears. You can tell yourself that those past pains and unfortunate experiences will not occur again, for nothing is quite the same the second time around.

The methods of self-hypnosis described so far will be effective in altering or removing the reflexes that are negative. In this chapter, we will read of other methods of direct hypnotic suggestions that do not involve inducing a trance state.

It is perfectly possible to sit down and discover just why you fear this, that or the other provided you are prepared to look back into the past and uncover the unhappy memories that now trigger off present difficulties. Some people cannot easily swallow a tablet because, at some time in the past, they tried swallowing one and nearly choked. Every time they now try the same thing, they find that the conditioned reflex action of the throat is to close up for fear of choking again. The self-hypnotist, without having to induce a trance state, will tell himself that this time the tablet *will* go down quickly and smoothly. With the tablet in his mouth, he will quickly visualise the tablet going smoothly and effortlessly down his throat. By concentrating he will see, in his mind's eye, the tablet sliding down perfectly. Swallowing water with it will help and the tablet *will* be swallowed easily. If not at the first attempt, then certainly at the second or third. After that, taking treatment would be automatic, because the first unpleasant experience will at last have been removed from the memory.

Here is a short list of negative conditioned reflexes that an individual can develop through past, unfortunate experiences. It may well be that you have experienced one or some of them. A similar circumstance can cause you to recall instantly the negative past and this will direct and control your immediate reactions.

PAST HAPPENINGS	CONDITIONED REFLEX NOW
1 Bitten by a dog	*Now fears all dogs*
2 Nearly drowned when first learning to swim	*Now cannot learn through fear of drowning*
3 Blushed when first introduced to a gathering of people	*Now fears crowds and socialising*
4 Failed physically on first sexual encounter	*Now avoids sexual contacts through fear of impotence or failure*
5 Had a near-accident in a car and cannot drive or be driven	*Now fears all methods of transport*
6 As a child, was fearful and made sick on a fairground swing	*Now fears sickness at sea, in an aeroplane or in a car*
7 Saw a dog/cat run over in a street	*Now cannot watch a dog/cat cross a road and has to go down a side road to avoid what might happen to an animal*

That illustrates just a very few instances where the mind assimilates, accumulates and recalls and then initiates a course of action because of what happened in the past.

The successful self-hypnotist can reject past bad impressions and experiences by auto-suggestive affirmations, even when not in a trance-state, that are in direct contradiction to the negative influences of the past. Bad memories can be eradicated and killed for all time by going out and facing them.

1 Stroke a dog and know he is not going to bite you.

2 Start to learn to swim because you will not drown.

3 Mingle in crowds and socialise, for this time you will not blush.

4 Use sex with real love and you will not fail.

5 Learn to drive or willingly ride in a car. There will be no accident.

6 You now have a strong stomach, you will not be sick.

7 Walk the streets calmly, animals know how to take care of themselves.

Many things that we do each day are involuntary. We digest food, excrete, blink, walk, talk, sit down, stand up, go to sleep. But, if we allow self-hypnotically induced negative suggestions to influence us results can be very unfortunate. We fear the worst and we *get* the worst, because we anticipate it.

FUNCTION	FEAR
1 Breathing	*We will develop palpitations and breathlessness.*
2 Digesting	*We will be sick, develop indigestion, even get an ulcer.*
3 Excreting	*We will get constipated, develop a blockage.*

4 Blinking	*We will develop a nervous 'tic' or spasm of the face.*
5 Walking	*We will stagger, stumble, trip over.*
6 Talking	*We will stammer, stutter, hesitate, get tongue-tied.*
7 Sit down	*We will develop cramp, find it difficult to rise.*
8 Stand up	*We will grow heavy, lose balance.*
9 Sleep	*We will develop insomnia.*

Those symptoms of ill-ease can be brought on by:

1 Worrying about the way we are breathing.

2 Thinking what we eat is bad or indigestible.

3 Thinking our bowels are not working correctly.

4 Concentrating on the ability to blink, being over-conscious of it.

5 Denying regular exercise as health-giving.

6 Being afraid to speak in public or in private in case we appear to be making fools of ourselves or saying the wrong things.

7 Sitting down thinking it will be difficult or awkward to rise again.

8 Standing up in front of people and fearing they are looking and making fun of us.

9 Letting the mind be too active at bed time or filled with anxiety thoughts.

All negative, worry thoughts! Being afraid of what *might* happen rather than concentrating on what can be *made* to happen by constructive, logical thinking.

In practising self-hypnosis, and, in the light of these demonstrations of the way in which you can bring about conditioned reflexes it must be realised and accepted that you *can* condition yourself to the good things in life, dismissing and disclaiming the bad things. It must also, by now, be apparent to you that, if you can negatively hypnotise yourself into accepting the *bad* things, you can also hypnotise yourself into an acceptivity state to realise the *good* things. You can, after practice, formulate conditioned reflexes that will command you to be receptive to all the positive auto-suggestive affirmations you put to yourself, either in an induced trance-state or off-the-cuff, so to speak.

You put yourself into a favourable state of mind to accept self-hypnotic suggestions by the associations of certain stimuli, the use of the bright white light, the close-up view of the reducing circles, the counting-method or the audio-method all of which have already been described. Setting the scene for those self-hypnotising sessions puts you into an immediate state of mind, associated with the first or second time you set the stage. Already, then, you are creating in your mind an acceptivity state and that is why all succeeding sessions grow ever more powerful and ultimately even more satisfactory.

It will be ideal, in creating this favourable state of mind, to condition yourself to a time, a place and a method, in order that your pliable mind gets to know and to act upon familiar stimuli and therefore slips more easily into an acceptivity state as to what is to follow. If it knows that the time will be six in the evening, the place, your bedroom and the method, the Audio or the Close-up, it will respond all the more quickly to what will have become an expected habit-pattern.

After each session of self-hypnosis, condition your mind to expect and to anticipate the next session. When the time arrives for it, your mind will be ready. Surround yourself with positive belief in the power of your hypnotic sessions and you will build a barrier between your mind and all negative outside suggestions that may intrude. It will be as if you are surrounded by an impenetrable 'wall' that outside influences just cannot lay seige to. You will be master of your mind, and it will no longer be something that can easily be influenced, either by others or by past negative impressions.

Accept that, when under your own hypnotic influence:

- **You are not a robot nor an automaton.**
- **You are completely relaxed.**
- **You are in full command of your faculties.**

Just think, you can often hear a clock ticking in your room but once you start to think of something else you no longer hear it. You have forgetten the existence of the clock, therefore you do not hear its ticking. In the same way, if you forget the negative sights, sounds and unpleasant impressions of the past you will not recall them. Not, that is, until you deliberately grow conscious of sights and sounds or past memories by your deliberate *attention* to them or by some association of ideas that resurrects them or makes you aware of their presence.

The time at which you wish to 'wake-up' from a self-hypnotic session is decided at the outset by telling yourself that, at the conclusion of the set number of auto-suggestions you are putting to yourself, you will come out of the trance-state. And you will! When you are having a bad dream or a nightmare you often hear yourself urging you to wake up or asking someone in your dream to wake you up. And you always *do* wake up because your conscious mind is taking control and disallowing your subconscious to have a hold over you any longer. So, with 'waking' from self-hypnosis your conscious mind tells you to wake up. You may even tell yourself that, on the count of five, you will come out of your trance state. This command, given at the beginning of your session, will be acted upon at the end of your session when you *do* count up to five. That is mind-mastery and *you* can have it with little effort, once your mind has learnt who *is* master.

10

Self-Induced Post-Hypnotic Suggestions

Post-hypnotic suggestions are ones to be thought of or carried out *after* a self-hypnotic session is over. Post-hypnotic suggestions can be carried out at any time after you have commanded them to take place.

Since the mind works on two planes, the conscious and the subconscious, it is easy to see that, remembering something during the day shows the subconscious at work. It is bringing to the conscious mind the relevant facts of the particular memory recall. If, before dropping off to sleep, you have been concentrating on a particular problem your subconscious mind will mull it over while you continue to sleep. When you wake up and start to live again on the higher plane of consciousness, the subconscious, on the lower plane, will provide the solution to the problem.

The sleepwalker can, by acting on impulses from his subconscious, get up, still asleep, perform a task dictated to him by his subconscious, then go back to bed and to sleep. Upon waking the next morning, he finds, much to his surprise that the job has been done. During the night he has 'lived' on the lower plane. Now, awake, he is on the higher plane of his conscious mind. Involuntary post-hypnotic instructions transmitted themselves to his subconscious while he was falling asleep and his subconscious determined to carry them out. But the non-sleepwalker waits until morning before he carries out the instructions.

It is vital that, before you give yourself post-hypnotic suggestive therapy, you determine exactly what you are going to suggest to yourself for future action. Here are some examples of post-hypnotic suggestions that may improve your waking hours and make life more pleasant and acceptable.

- *Cigarettes are going to taste dreadful to me from now on.*

- *I am going to start to feel ill if I drink more than two pints of beer.*
- *My daily headaches at work are going to stop right now.*
- *I am not going to be a nervous wreck at my interview with Mr So-and-so.*
- *The exam will be simple. I will know all the answers to all the questions.*
- *I will not allow money worries to get me down any more as from today.*
- *I will have the courage to say what I want to say, without hesitation.*
- *As a performer, I am going to sweep the audience off its feet!*
- *As a salesman I am going to get that large order I am after.*
- *I am going to pass my next driving test easily.*
- *I am going to have the courage to fight all opposition to me.*
- *I will be a real success at the party tonight.*
- *Today, I will not give way to any silly feelings about my health. I am fit.*
- *I am independent now. I no longer have to look to anyone for anything.*

You should find it an easy task to adapt these auto-suggestions for post-hypnotic effect to suit your own requirements. In your trance state, induced by any of the methods so far suggested, make a point of detailing the time, the day, the evening, the night – even the week, in which you want your subconscious to bring the suggestions up into your conscious mind to influence and control your actions and thoughts according to the commands you have given.

If a trained hypnotist can implant into your subconscious certain thoughts and actions to be carried out upon waking from a trance, then, inevitably, *you* can implant powerful ideas and post-hypnotic suggestions into your mind with every confidence they will work.

When a subject is being put in a trance by a hypnotist the subject is in reality hypnotising *himself* into being hypnotised! The job is almost done by the time the therapist faces his subject. It is not, merely, the hypnotist who does the hypnotising; *you,* too, are willing or hypnotising yourself into being put into a trance! That is well illustrated by the subject who just cannot be hypnotised by a therapist against his will, because he has not self-hypnotised himself into *wanting* to 'go under'.

But you have only yourself to contend with. You want to hypnotise yourself and so you will! Do accept that statement as an undeniable fact.

11

The Brow-Stroke Method

This is a very personal method of inducing self-hypnosis. It is personal because it involves linking yourself up *with* yourself. In other words, it is completing a circuit similar to the linking-up of positive and negative poles to produce a flow of electricity.

In a spiritual séance, participants sit round a table and link hands with each other so that a powerful circle of force is formed. Each person thinks of exactly the same thing while hands are linked. The result is that the idea of one individual to get through to the 'other side' is magnified many times. The effect, therefore, is that the 'idea' becomes one big thought, larger by far than if it were conjured up by just one person.

In this Brow-stroke method, you are going to link yourself up with yourself so that your auto-suggestive affirmations become magnified two-fold.

Consider your right hand to be positive and your left hand to be negative. To set your subconscious mind in action, a circuit (positive and negative) has to be completed as would an electric circuit have to be completed to light up a lamp.

In this instance, *you* are the electric lamp and your subconscious mind is 'lit-up' by joining your right and your left hands together. However, the 'switch-on' is not accomplished until you place your joined hands onto your forehead.

To do this, sit at a table with your elbows resting on the edge of it. Interlock the four fingers of each hand together and press them against your forehead – allowing your two thumbs to splay out, pressing on both temples. Your head should be facing downwards.

Pressing your fingers hard against your forehead and your thumbs firmly against your temples, close your eyes. The 'circuit' is now completed and you have 'switched' yourself on. Conjure up a picture of an electric lamp and concentrate on the brilliance of the filament. Think hard of the white, hot light you see when you stare straight at a lighted bulb.

When you have formed this bright image in your mind, imagine, with all your might, that the bright white light is your subconscious mind and that you are staring straight at it inside your head.

Having predetermined your auto-suggestive affirmations, start to move your head slowly from left to right, right to left, left to right and so on, while at the same time, keeping up the pressure as your fingers and thumbs pass over the hard surface of the forehead and the temples.

Now start to give yourself the auto-suggestions, repeating each one several times as you move your head from left to right and back again.

Try to keep up this motion of the head, this pressure of the fingers and the thumbs for ten minutes, while your elbows are still resting on the table.

After a very short while, you will begin to feel you are floating in space, that your head is divorced from your body and that the white light (your subconscious) is burning into your eyes.

You can speak directly *to* your subconscious. Instead of saying, in your normal voice: 'I am going to do this, that or the other', address your subconscious mind directly: '*You* are going to do this, that or the other. *You* are going to make me go there. *You* are going to give me courage. *You* are going to stop me from being nervous. *You* are going to make me strong and forthright in all I do and in all I say. *You* will not allow me to be defeated, weak-willed, ineffectual, sensitive, over-emotional', and so on, according to the positive powers you wish to acquire, your aims in life, your strong desires to overcome adversity and people who try to dominate you.

As with other methods, practise this often until you find it really starting to be effective. Very favourable times for this and other methods so far described are near bed time, when the conscious mind is beginning to feel pleasantly drowsy and the body is growing tired and ready for rest. The sleep which should follow will give the subconscious mind even more time to work upon and take in the affirmations you have put in to it.

When you have finished this Brow-stroke method, unclasp your fingers, open your eyes, get accustomed to the light in the room and the familiar surroundings again. Let your arms drop to your sides while you are still in a sitting position at the table.

Do not rise from the table hastily. You have now broken the positive-negative circuit within your body and your mind. You have switched off. If it *is* bed time, go to bed. If not, relax in an armchair and, if you feel drowsy give way to it. Even a short nap will help your subconscious mind to absorb further all you have said to it.

12

The Hypno-Dynamic Method

Hypno means a trance state, dynamic describes an effective, forceful personality or an effective force.

When you are faced with an important interview that may mean a great deal to you, or when you know you will have to make an extra effort to impress someone there are dynamic powers within you that you can bring to the surface to help you win through.

These dynamic powers that most of us possess often only manifest themselves when we lose our temper and flare up in a verbal or physical confrontation. Even though some of us may feel rather meek and mild in our dealings with everyday matters and prefer to present an affable front to those we mix with, there is a fighting force lurking deep down inside. We can, if we wish, bring it to the surface in times of stress when challenged by people or circumstances that call for a show of power on our part.

In a crisis, the adrenalin glands get to work and we are possessed by the idea of running away or standing our ground. The latter impulse, to face up and fight, is, of course, the dynamic force coming into play.

At times, though, when having to make a snap decision or face a crisis that demands quick thinking and speedy action, we find this force is too far down in the subconscious to be brought to the surface quickly enough to come to our rescue.

Using the Hypno-dynamic method of self-hypnosis before a vital meeting, before an important test, before a decision of paramount importance has to be made, can be of great value.

Dealing now with a non-spectacular situation before it takes place, but knowing it is inevitable and very important to personal progress, you can use the Hypno-dynamic method in the quiet of your room and in the quiet of your mind. It involves an indulgence in fantasies that take you out of your normal, conventional existence for a short while and send your mind whirling away on planes that you know you do not really have to reach, but the fictional realisation of them puts you into a state of 'over-wind' for a while. In effect, you wind yourself up in your imagination far beyond the demands of the actual crisis you have to face. The effect is that later, when you come face-to-face with the interviewer, the employer, the partner you wish to succeed with, your 'over-wind' has wound down somewhat, but still retains enough dynamic tension and effectiveness to help you to win through.

This is the procedure:

---

1 The day before you have to cope with the dreaded confrontation, lie flat on your bed and stare up at the ceiling. Now start to fantasise. Choose those things you would like to do that are closest to your heart and that have probably been unfulfilled ambitions in your adult life. Dispense, in your mind, with all ifs and buts and accept that everything *is* possible.

---

2 Let yourself float away thinking of all the fantastic things in life you would just love to do.

---

3 Think big and talk big. *Be* that celebrated actor, that famous concert pianist, that successful artist, that infamous womaniser. Think of being a millionaire spending, spending, spending!

---

4 Think of your repressions: you are no longer repressed. Think of your inhibitions: you are no longer inhibited.

---

5 Travel the world. Go to all those places seen only in travel brochures that you have never been able to visit. Sell cars, real estate, computers, whatever you are most interested in. Be the managing director of a large corporation.

---

6 Whirl yourself away on an incredible fantasy of wishful-thinking at last realised because *now* you have everything and everyone under your own, powerful, dominant control.

---

7 Having fantasised yourself into the impossible, start to focus your attention on the great goal that lies ahead of you to-

morrow. You are in the same euphoric mood and the interview is taking place. You own the world and it has owed you a living and now you are going to get it. Nothing will stop you now. Tomorrow when you face your interviewer you will have the situation in hand. You have scaled the heights in your fantasy world, now go ahead and transfer all those positive thoughts into the situation that faces you. Think big and you will *be* big. Remember the power of positive projection as you face your opponent. As you thought big in that conscious trance-state yesterday, so do the same now. Project this confident thinking as you look your protagonist straight between the eyes at his weakest facial point.

8 Think of yourself as larger than life and the person facing you as small and insignificant. Get yourself into a self-induced trance state now as you look at the person facing you. When he speaks, listen but, at the same time, *will* your dynamic thoughts to him and at him. (*You like me. I impress you. You like my confidence, my personality.*)

9 If an important interview is weeks ahead, give yourself this Hypno-dynamic treatment every day or every night right up until the night before the vital meeting. Boost yourself up over and over again, many, many times. Soon, you will come to believe in yourself more than ever before. Your flights of fancy will make you realise that most things that can be visualised *can* be *realised*. And the most important thing to understand is that your vital hopes can be realised by your personal dynamism, a state of mind to which you have now conditioned yourself by those Hypno-dynamic sessions, and by a positive frame of mind.

10 People who talk money often make money, lots of it. People who talk big often become big. Hypno-dynamic sessions can so invigorate you that, when the important time arrives, you subconsciously recall and react to the larger than life suggestions you have conjured up.

Do try it – often! It could work wonders for you if you believe in it entirely.

13

Your Second Self

Most people are mildly schizophrenic in the nicest possible way. That is, they are not a menace to themselves nor to society. The two sides of you are well-illustrated if you look at a portrait of yourself and cover one half of the photograph. One side of your face seems to have a slight glint in the eye and possibly a smile on the mouth. Cover the other side of the photograph and the difference can be quite remarkable. The eye looks more solemn, perhaps more closed than the other and the mouth seems to have a downward droop.

The first side of your face you looked at shows the happy, good-humoured side of your nature. The opposite side shows the more solemn, moody side.

Try it!

Or you can look at your face in a mirror, covering each side in turn, and see the differences in your facial expressions.

Every face does not, by any means, show the same distribution of happiness or solemnity.

Since cameras rarely lie, we can take this interesting division of natures as shown in facial expressions to be genuine. And this surely indicates the presence, in each one of us, of two people! One, happy, carefree and lighthearted; the other, serious, thoughtful, perhaps even cunning.

The second self that we all have within us is known as the Alter Ego, the alternative 'I Am'. The Other Person. The happy Ego says, 'smile in the face of adversity,' but the serious, thoughtful or even antagonistic Ego says, 'fight, oppose, threaten, hit out!'. So inner conflict can arise, in which the two selves vie with each other as to what decision is to be taken in a crisis.

Most people manage to be in control of their Alter Ego and the right actions are taken, the right ideas arrived at and the right things said.

The happy person, however, may allow him/herself to be

dominated in a crisis by his/her antagonistic Alter Ego. On the other hand, the antagonistic person is pleased to allow his or her happy Alter Ego to take command in a crisis. Few people recognise the presence of a second self, an Alter Ego, and are, therefore, often at variance with themselves and allow the wrong Ego to take command.

Extending this premise a little further, think of the old wives' adage that talking to oneself is the 'first sign of madness'. Certainly, among the genuinely mentally disturbed, people *do* talk to themselves, for this is a safety-valve. But thousands of perfectly well-balanced individuals talk to themselves regularly, either by talking audibly, or by 'thinking' their thoughts to themselves. In the normal, healthy and mentally-fit person, this is by no means a 'first sign of madness'. It is, in fact, a very good indication of sanity!

Talking to oneself is an acknowledgement, however unwitting, of the presence of a second-self, an Alter Ego. Very often, the person who does not talk to himself, audibly or mentally flies off the handle at the slightest excuse, says the wrong things at the wrong times, thinks the wrong thoughts and takes wrong steps in negative situations.

If you are not in the habit of talking to yourself, reasoning out problems and situations, you are quite likely the sort of person who takes precipitate action, makes unwise, on-the-spot decisions, utters unfortunate remarks, flares up quickly without reasonable thought.

Many loners, only children, anti-social individuals, talk to themselves as a means of compensation for lack of brothers and sisters in childhood or because of an unhappy home environment or through a deep-rooted sense of inferiority.

Let it be understood that by talking to yourself you are entering into a mild self-hypnotic state that creates a situation of companionship, whether one is leading a happy life or whether one is, in fact, a loner. It is a communication with one's second self that so very often can be invaluable in preventing nervous debility, breakdowns or psychosomatic disorders.

Just think of it! You cannot fall out with yourself! You cannot argue with yourself, but you *can* reason. You need never be alone if you are in communication with yourself.

The self-hypnotically induced acceptance that you are never alone can be a tremendous boost to morale on occasions. It is entirely possible, by this form of self-induced suggestion, to actually 'see', in your mind's eye, the second self to whom you are speaking. Last thing at night, especially before dropping off to sleep, a conversation with yourself about the affairs of the day and the hopes for further achievement tomorrow can feed good, positive thoughts into the subconscious to be favourably acted upon tomorrow. Often, it is more than a good thing to say 'We' rather than 'I' when making an important decision or trying to rid yourself of a bad habit. Instead of saying, 'I will give up smoking', it is good to take your second self into your confidence and say, 'We will give up smoking'. If an unpleasant thought occurs it is good to say, 'We will not think of that now'. If you are in the uncomfortable position of needing a loo but cannot find one it is helpful to say, 'We don't want to go now'! The conspiracy between the two selves can really work wonders. In hypnotising yourself into knowing you have an ever-present companion with whom you will never fall out, you can arm yourself against flesh-and-blood opposition on many occasions.

14

The Hypno-Calm Method

Do not underestimate nor dismiss the idea of using the 'We' instead of the 'I' identification when giving self-hypnotic suggestions, particularly if you *are* prone to talk to yourself from time to time. It may seem slightly strange at first, but talking to yourself is not, as some folk would probably have it, an eccentricity. The 'We', used by the individual in this context, gives an extra proportion to suggestive-therapy in that it creates a feeling, in the individual, of an invisible friend or companion who lends sterling support in times of need. In any case, if you sensibly accept the fact that there *is* a second-self within you, an Alter Ego, then you need not be abashed at the thought of using this second self to assist you in your problems. Queen Victoria, in her famous pronouncement that, 'We are not amused' gave additional weight to her opinion by creating an invisible circle of disapproving partners simply by the power of suggestion. You can do the same for yourself and, in so doing, add strength and conviction to your auto-suggestive therapy.

In Chapter 12, we examined the Hypno-dynamic method for self-hypnosis. The purpose of that particular technique is to help you to measure up to a crisis by inducing positive powers in your mind to strengthen your resolve to win through.

Now we will examine the Hypno-calm method, designed to bring you *down* from a crisis point and, in fact, to calm you again. It is a question of mental and emotional tranquillisers – the 'uppers' and the 'downers'.

Often, when success has been achieved, a job secured or an ambition realised, euphoria sets in for a while, causing a state of excitability and restlessness, robbing a person of sleep, creating slight confusion of mind and, in some cases raising blood-pressure and causing breathlessness, palpitations and so on. These symptoms do, in fact, disappear eventually, but sometimes not as quickly as you would like. The Hypno-calm method is designed to assist a speedy descent from exhilaration to a normal acceptance of a situation, whether it is a happy or a sad one. It is an 'after-the-ball-is-over' period in which pleasure is reviewed in retrospect and put in proper proportion and perspective.

Hypno means a trance-state.

Calm describes peace-of-mind, tranquility, happiness in successful endeavour.

Hypno-calm then describes the calm personality or the calming influence.

This is the procedure:

1 Lie flat on your bed in a darkened room. Relax completely from toes to head, commanding your nervous energy to flow gently away from your body until you feel pleasantly limp, even a little drowsy.

2 Get your possibly confused, but happy, thoughts back into neat order. Bodily and emotional relaxation is vital in the aftermath of a crisis or the realisation of a longed-for ambition. This you now succeed in achieving by letting your body 'melt away' and your mind become becalmed.

3 Stare up at the ceiling. Replace, in your mind, the starkness of the ceiling with floating clouds. Imagine you are drifting upwards towards them.

4 Now recall, slowly and luxuriously the events at that interview or confrontation that resulted in your complete and absolute triumph over adversity or aggression. Mull over in your mind the gradual turning-of-the-tables in your favour. The things you said. The things you did. The positive points you made. Delight in them. Feel exalted. Rerun the mental film over and over again until you are able to accept the circumstances calmly.

5 Gradually come down from the clouds again, feeling calm, cool and collected in your thoughts. Begin to resolve the pleasant turn of events into practical, present moves that you know will help you get the very best out of the conditions that now prevail.

6 In your own measured time, get up from the bed and restoring the full light by opening the curtains or switching on the lights, accept the suddenly renewed brilliance as the personification of your success. You have won through! The trials and tribulations of yesterday are no more. This is *today* – the beginning of a new life for you.

The Hypno-calm method, tried more than once, if necessary, will go more than a long way to restore your equilibrium in times of happy, excited 'stress' and will bring you down to earth again in the nicest possible way. Ready, now, to make the most of your new opportunities of success and achievement, with an unclouded and an uncomplicated mind and attitude. It will not be the calm before the storm, but the calm before the sunshine.

15

Protect Yourself Against Other People's Suggestions

Positive hetero-suggestion (what people say to you about you) can be good, and good advice must be acted upon, not dismissed because your Ego feels hurt.

But negative hetero-suggestion can be harmful if you allow it to influence you to a degree that causes you to mistrust yourself, to lose faith in yourself and to make you try to readjust your life according to how *others* think it should be run. You must develop the courage of your own convictions, not the convictions of others if they are obviously bad for you.

- **People may be spitefully disposed to you.**
- **They may give you bad advice in order to impede your progress.**
- **They may attempt to make you feel ill when you are well.**
- **They may try to give you a wrong impression of yourself by hurtful criticism and insulting remarks as to face or figure.**
- **Or they may falsely flatter you to give you an exaggerated impression of yourself.**
- **They may suggest you are a failure or they may place you in a fool's paradise that misleads and misguides you.**
- **They may try to discount your true abilities and capabilities.**
- **They may try to smother you by false or hypocritical emotionalism.**
- **They may attack your weakest and most vulnerable mental and physical spots.**
- **They may attempt to remould your personality.**
- **They may try to make you feel inferior.**

And, who *are* 'they'?

They are your relatives, your family, your friends, your work associates, your social companions, newly discovered 'friends'. All with some motive to beat you down for some reason or another.

These people are intent on sowing the seeds of negative hetero-suggestions into your mind, mainly to belittle you, to triumph over you or to adapt you to their own wishes in order to be able to use you for their own ends.

You must protect yourself against them all.

There are embittered, disappointed, unsuccessful, frustrated, inhibited and repressed people who seek to demoralise those around them in order to hide or to compensate for their own inadequacies.

Some negative suggestions from others are not vindictive in intent. *Some* people actually do try to be constructive in criticism, but it is so often thoughtless and ill-timed.

It is very easy to be swayed and influenced by outside suggestions that tend to de-personalise and to rob you of your dignity and positive opinion of yourself.

The evil menace of gossip can come creeping in on a person's life in an indirect fashion: 'He said to me and I said to him and someone else passed it on', and, eventually, it gets to *you*. It is rumour, hearsay, scandal-mongering. The talk of defeatists, escapists from the realities of life.

But it gets to *you*.

All this negativism starts in other people's minds. But why should it be allowed to affect *your* mind?.

Watch a television programme you don't like. You switch it off, or change to another, more acceptable channel.

Listen to a radio programme that bores you and you switch off or change to another, more pleasant wave-length.

Listen to the adverse, negative suggestions from an individual and, if you do not like it, switch to a more companionable person.

No one should allow their mind to be influenced by the mind of another person.

Neither should *you* allow your mind to be occupied by the negative suggestions from others that affect your own thoughts or your opinion of yourself. You, too, can switch off or turn to another, more positive 'thought-wave-length'.

What you wish and choose to reject, your mind will reject and refuse for you. You can absolutely blot out negative suggestions by positive auto-suggestions.

Some people love to receive and accept destructive, negative suggestions because they are masochists. The more their feelings are hurt, the more they like it because it helps them to follow their escapist attitude and gives them good reason for running away from life. 'So-and-So said this, that and the other and it *must* be true so I do not have to make any efforts to contradict it.'

But, radio and television-wise, you can jam all outside interference of a negative nature and instead, get positive reception and a clear picture.

Some people block out disasters and unfortunate happenings by self-induced refusal to acknowledge such things. This is a very mild form of amnesia, in which the mind forgets unpleasant crises and sometimes never resurrects them. Self-induced 'amnesia' is by no means as deep or as effective as the genuine state of mind caused by an horrific accident, a fearful sight or a devastating experience. Nevertheless, a refusal to acknowledge something unpleasant can very often be most effective. A girl may blot out the circumstances of a rape because she is too horrified to acknowledge that it has happened to her. A man may refuse to believe he has committed a crime because he cannot believe he was capable of doing it.

Equally, and in a far less dramatic way, an individual can blot out and refuse to remember an unfortunate incident that upset his or her peace of mind. That would be an involuntary action on the part of that person's mind because the thinking processes would have automatically thrust the negative circumstance deep down into the subconscious, incapable of conscious recollection until possibly jolted by a sudden association of ideas or by psychotherapy.

However, this quite merciful blanking-out of a negative occurrence cannot *always* be achieved automatically by the mind. It is then, of course, that auto-suggestions become invaluable. Not necessarily to blot out the situation, but to refuse to allow it to affect present moves. The unpleasant memory will not be declared null-and-void. Instead, it will be discounted, diminished, dissolved.

Because, by employing at least one of the self-hypnotic methods so far described, *you will have told yourself that that is so.*

If you are told you are looking ill, say, 'I am not ill'.

If you are told you will probably not get that job, say, 'I mean to get that job'.

Say whatever is appropriate to the case, not only to yourself, but to the person who is confronting you as well.

Telling yourself is good, telling your protagonist is excellent because, as you utter the positive affirmations out loud, your opponent is taken off guard, and in an effort to hide his confusion and embarrassment, will probably counter his negative suggestion by hastily contradicting it. In that way, you may well receive a positive suggestion on his part that confirms your own convictions and further implants your positive outlook into your subconscious.

It is not just a battle of wits, it is a battle of minds.

When someone enters your home without asking, this is an invasion of your privacy.

When someone 'enters' your mind without invitation, this is an invasion of your mental and emotional privacy. Refute those negative suggestions and add:

- *'No, as a matter of fact, I feel in perfect health. Very fit, actually.'*
- *'I have every hope of getting that job. I have all the capabilities called for on the application form, so I really don't see myself failing.*

Tell him! He or she can't just stand there, facing you and repeating negative remarks!

Another thing, don't be too influenced by negative suggestions made in newspapers, on radio, on television. Sensation sells and crisis headlines raise circulation. Journalism is a word-game and journalists often scare the wits out of readers, listeners and viewers. Rumours can also destroy peace of mind. Something alarming printed on the front page in black banner headlines is most likely reduced to one small inconsequential paragraph in another newspaper. You have been taken in by sensationalism. It is press policy and power politics that have scared you.

Suggestible people swayed unduly by anxiety brought on by negative hetero-suggestion from the media and other people become fearful of:

- **Losing their money.**
- **Being unemployed.**

- **Getting behind with mortgages and credit payments.**
- **Losing their homes.**
- **Losing husbands/wives.**
- **Losing their children.**
- **Missing out on popularity and prestige.**
- **Losing male virility/female fertility.**
- **Facing up to illness and/or death.**

Those negative fears can result in loss of dignity, pride, power, principles, faith, health and personal liberty.

You can lose the lot by listening to and accepting outside negative suggestions from others to destroy your hopes, your ambitions, your love-life.

Don't be one of those people always expecting the worst to happen. This attitude so often actually *does* attract the worst. As money makes money, so, undoubtedly, trouble makes trouble.

Possibly you wake each morning with a heavy heart and a leaden outlook. Will what went wrong yesterday go wrong again today? Yesterday is often the first thing you think about when you wake and collect your senses. 'What mistakes did I make? Did I lose money, make money? Did I get through that pile of work or am I behind? Will I get caught up again in that same old traffic jam on the way to work?'

Mercifully, after a while, you will find that your muddled and confused thinking is sorting itself out and you are beginning to see things in their proper proportions. Worry-thoughts in the subconscious are fading away and positive, conscious thoughts are taking over. That is the time to start to fill your mind with powerful positive auto-suggestions as you get ready to leave for your job, and while you are on your journey.

- *Today will be good and progressive.*
- *I will easily catch up on that workload.*
- *Nothing can or will go wrong today.*
- *If there is more money to be made I will make it.*
- *I will not worry if I am caught up in a traffic jam.*

Think these thoughts. Say them to yourself, many times, silently and convincingly. Get to your place of work in a positive state of mind.

Make this your Personal Formula for a Successful Day:
(Say it at breakfast and on your journey to work.)

- *I will overcome all opposition today.*
- *I will make the most of all that today has to offer me.*
- *I will enjoy every moment of today.*
- *I will show more consideration to others today.*
- *I will try to increase my mental awareness today.*

There is another attitude of negative hetero-suggestion that many people throw out in a denigrating, supercilious manner, in an attempt to promote their own imagined superiority.

For instance, on the subject of boredom, some folk think it is sophisticated to suggest that others must be bored by certain things, indicating that they are, so they must have a superior intelligence.

They may say:

- *'Aren't you bored all day long at home/or office?'*
- *'Surely that monotonous job must bore you?'*
- *'Doesn't he/she bore you?'*
- *'Don't they bore you?'*
- *'That film/play/television programme will bore you!*
- *'Don't read that book, you will be bored to tears!*

Such individuals will be pleased if you admit to the particular boredom they have singled out for you. But you can confound them by saying: 'No. This/that/the other most certainly does not bore *me*. I am rather surprised *you* get bored!'

They will quickly deflate!

You have instantly robbed them of their imagined sophistication and their superior attitudes and have placed yourself on a genuinely superior plane.

Don't curry favour by agreeing with them, either for the sake of peace or in an effort to place yourself on their imagined plane of sophistication.

They direct negative hetero-suggestions at *you*. You, in turn, direct positive hetero-suggestions at them with the result they begin to doubt themselves.

Even if you *are* bored by certain things and certain people, do not admit it to others who may question you. Unless, of course, common sense dictates that you *should* agree – to your own benefit.

Otherwise, tell them how much *they* bore *you*.

Finally, why do you become victim to what others say to, or about you?

Because:

1 You have a negative attitude towards yourself that automatically expects and accepts adverse criticism and suggestion.
2 You may well suffer from a general conviction of failure in yourself your abilities, your accomplishments in life and your inability to mix.
3 You *expect* antagonistic and negative suggestions to be levelled at you.

Think about it, and resolve to combat future negative hetero-suggestions.

16

The Mirror Method

This is a good method in which to use the 'We' commands instead of the 'I' commands. The basis of this particular method of inducing self-hypnosis and instilling positive auto-suggestions is to visualise the second-self, mentioned earlier.

Invariably we carry about with us an unseen image of ourselves that we imagine is a way in which others see us. From time to time, we look at ourselves in a mirror to check up on appearance, dress, tidiness and so on. Those few glances during the day give us true reflections of how we look and more or less remind us of the fact that we do, actually exist, apart from the senses of hearing, smelling, and touching, that give us the feeling of being alive.

The Mirror method is devised to bring us into intimate contact with ourselves for the purpose of registering auto-suggestions in our subconscious mind that have a powerful impact, because we are *looking* at ourselves during the session.

The technique is as follows.

Use a small square or oblong mirror and place it on some books on a table. Sit in an upright chair at the table and prop the mirror up in front of your face so that, when leaning forward comfortably on your elbows, you can gaze into it. But, and most importantly, ensure that you can see only your *eyes* and no other part of your face.

Having seated yourself comfortably as described in a degree of close up that does not distort your vision or put your eyes out of focus, dwell upon the fact that you are addressing your second-self, your Alter Ego. There are two of you.

As with all self-hypnotic sessions, before starting you must determine precisely what problem it is you need to put into perspective, what positive commands you want to give to yourself and to your second-self.

Having, therefore, predetermined them, gaze intently at the eyes that are gazing back at you. Induce warm feelings of closeness, togetherness, companionship with the 'person' into whose eyes you are looking so intently. Important agreements are now to be made between you both. You are about to agree, positively, on certain things to be said or actions to be taken for the ultimate betterment of you both. Fantasise on this until you begin to accept that you are not alone but have powerful support and cooperation to make things be what you most desire them to be.

With these firm convictions in mind, and staring with concentration at your own eyes, you will start to feel just that little bit drowsy. You will blink, as usual but you must make every effort to keep your eyes open. When you have conquered the slight drowsiness and it has settled down to that pleasant, pre-sleep sensation you experience at bedtime, commence your auto-suggestive commands and affirmations based on the programme you have previously decided upon.

Remember to use the 'We' instead of the 'I'.

As if in a pleasant conversation, and in modulated tones, speak to your image.

- *We are not going to blush every time we enter a crowded room.*
- *We are not going to get a headache every time we have a problem.*
- *We are not going to stammer or to stutter when speaking.*
- *We are not going to let So-and-So get the better of us.*
- *We are not going to feel ill when faced with anxiety.*
- *We are not going to allow our bad temper to rise in a crisis.*
- *We are not going to give way to our pet dread, fear, hate or aversion.*
- *We are not going to lie awake all night because of worry.*

. . . and so on according to your planned programme. If there is only one, particular, dominant suggestion you want to implant into your second self, dwell on it and emphasise it over and over again, for as long as you can.

You are not talking to yourself.

You are talking to the self *within* yourself.

Your second self is taking it all in, and when the vital moment arises in the future, your second self will remind you of the bond you have established, the promises you have made between the two of you, and the real *you* will respond and carry out those commands.

You will not want to look yourself straight in the eyes again and have to say:

'We failed ourselves, didn't we?'

Try this most valued and well-proven method of getting in touch with yourself. It can really work wonders.

17

Daily Training for Successful Self-Hypnosis

Auto and hetero-suggestion, acceptivity, suggestibility, pliability and malleability are inborn characteristics of the normal, healthy and mentally stable man and woman.

The all-powerful play and influence of words is always with us. All life depends upon things that are said, expressions used, phrases repeated. Nothing is done and nothing is accomplished in silence. Everything is attended by words which are the expression of thoughts.

The way in which ideas are conveyed from outside sources to the individual prompt positive or negative actions and reactions.

The way in which ideas are conveyed to you by *yourself* prompt positive or negative action on your part.

What you say to others influences them either positively or negatively. And what they say to you has a similar effect.

If you are determined to acquire the ability to practise self-hypnosis to better your life and give you a happier, more confident personality, it will be an advantage to train yourself in the art of concentration so that, when a self-hypnotic session is taking place, you are already conditioned to the task of narrowing down your conscious thoughts to such a degree that it is second nature to you to be able to shut out all peripheral visual images and all superflous thoughts and concentrate on the suggestions to be absorbed into the subconscious.

Choose a small, bright object such as a shiny tablespoon, a small mirror or a white saucer and place it on a table. Stand up and gaze down at it for some considerable time until you feel the space around you and the space around the object becoming brighter and brighter and the immediate surroundings become darker until they are almost out of sight. You may well take up to ten or fifteen minutes initially to accomplish this. With perseverance, it will come about. Concentrate all your thoughts upon the bright object. This is not a self-hypnotic session, it is an exercise to accustom you to focus your eyes and mind on one given object for a length of time, so strengthening your eyes, your patience and your power of intense concentration.

This exercise, carried out at least once or twice a day, will soon condition your eyes to focus firmly and your thoughts to become directed to one thought alone – the bright object.

Another successful excercise is to stick a small circle of very white paper in the centre of a wardrobe or a dressing-table mirror. Standing near to the mirror get the circle of white paper well into focus. You will see the reflection of your face round the circumference of the white circle. Gaze long at the white circle, willing yourself to lose sight of the image of your face. See it fade into misty obscurity – together with the reflections of the room behind you until all you are aware of is the circle of white paper. You can use this process for actual self-hypnotic inducement if you wish.

Try that exercise several times until it is a reflex action on your part to 'dissolve' your face and all reflected surroundings in the mirror in favour of the one object before you – the circle of white paper.

This exercise helps you to channel your thoughts on one thing at a given time and is essential for creating the correct atmosphere for successful self-hypnosis.

Given that you have good eyesight, another exercise is to stare at a naked electric light for several minutes on end, until the surrounding area becomes darkened and your eyes smart a bit. Then take your gaze away and concentrate on the black image of the light bulb you will see in front of your eyes until it fades away. Only try this once a day for a short time.

Out walking, in a park for instance, focus your eyes on a distant object as you walk and try to dismiss all other objects surrounding you until the distant object is all that you can see and are aware of.

Practise inducing deep relaxation before dropping off to sleep at night. *Will* your body to become limp and liquid from the toes up, slowly making your muscles relax, visualising the process taking place as the pleasurable sensation creeps up from your toes until legs, torso and arms are completely loose. See, in your mind's eye, waves of relaxation creeping up like the soft waves on a sea shore.

Regulated breathing exercises help, too.

In front of an open window breathe in, count to five, expel.

Again – now counting to nine, expel.

Again – trying for a count of twelve or more, expel.

These breathing sessions will help you to develop rhythm in breathing and will help you to bring about complete relaxation of body and mind.

18

The Mind Explained

The brain is a very tangible object, a mass of nerves and countless cells, the entire structure cleverly balanced within the casing of the skull. A heavy blow to the head, as with a professional boxer can shift the brain within the structure of the skull so severely that the fighter can suffer permanent brain damage. The same can be the result of a car accident or any misfortune that brings about severe brain damage. The brain more or less 'floats' in a fluid within the skull so it is vulnerable and can easily be put off balance.

The 'mind' is the magical manifestation of thoughts transmitted from the brain to the body, sending messages of pain, fright, fear, exultation, and so on.

The body reacts and behaves according to the dictates of the mind manufactured in the brain-cells. If you cut your finger and see it happening, your mind at once sends a message to your finger to start to experience pain. *And you do*. That applies to most injuries that are seen to happen. However, if you are unaware that you have cut your finger, the mind does not send out messages to feel pain. A little while later, though, you notice the cut and the dried blood around it and you realise you have cut your finger. This sudden awareness is picked up by your brain which at once sends a message to your finger to start feeling pain.

A soldier can easily receive a superficial wound in the arm or the leg and not, in the heat of conflict, be aware of it immediately. Later, when he realises he has been shot, the mind tells him to start to feel pain. *And he does*.

These are just two small examples of the tricks the brain and the mind can play on us.

Indian Fakirs who step on red-hot coals, or lie on a bed of nails, refuse to let messages of pain be transmitted to their feet or to their bodies and, so great is their triumph over the mind, that they just do *not* feel pain. They indulge in a self-hypnotic state that blocks out pain by auto-suggestion that pain does not exist.

Having perhaps suffered a very serious accident resulting in much pain the patient later will not remember the accident nor the pains suffered as a result. His mind deliberately blocks out all memory, because he *refuses* to remember it and does not wish to remember either the accident or the agony that followed. This is a merciful function of the brain and the mind and generally helps towards the complete recovery of the patient. This 'magical' process is called amnesia, total loss of memory about a particular episode.

It does not only occur in cases of the blotting-out of pain. It can also effectively shut out memories of a crime committed, a tragic bereavement, something dreadful happening to a loved-one or feelings of guilt. By not remembering, one cannot be *accused*. By forgetting, one can be *excused*.

But doctors and psychiatrists know all about that, of course, and where guilt is felt as a result of a crime committed, the truth drug or hypnosis itself can be used to drag the truth up from the subconscious into the conscious and in that way aid prompt recall. When a memory is too painful to resurrect and no crime is involved, it is left to rest so that the patient is not forced to relive the situation which might well affect the rest of his or her life.

The creative self-hypnotist may as well have a briefing on a few states of mind that he is heir to. Knowing about them will no doubt help him to recognise and overcome them, should they occur. They will not then easily subvert his happiness and progress in life.

These are a few of the negative states of mind that so easily affect the average individual. Knowing about them may well assist you in controlling them so that they are not allowed to interfere with your desire to enlist the aid of self-hypnosis in times of stress.

Conversion neurosis	A worry turned into an illness.
Return to Infantilism	A childish attitude to problems in order to escape finding a solution.
Obsessions	Fixed ideas that common sense cannot dismiss.

Inhibitions	Mental 'brakes' that are put on normal, everyday actions.
Compulsions	Fixed feelings that certain actions must be taken, otherwise things will go wrong for you.
Anxiety Neurosis	Unreasonable worry about the most ordinary things, conditions, circumstances and situations.
Introversion	A desire to withdraw from life, from family, from society. Looking inwards instead of looking outside yourself. The Introvert. The opposite is the Extrovert, the person who is outgoing.
Schizophrenia	A serious illness. It results in 'split personality' in serious cases but in ordinary, everyday ways, a general sense of recurring moodiness and depression alternating with joy and possible euphoria.

Happily, the average well-balanced person, like yourself, does not get affected by such mental and emotional upheavals.

That short list may help to alleviate certain worries and so prevent psychosomatic illnesses from occurring. These imaginary aches and pains give us a reason for not doing things we find difficult or distasteful. Recognising possible stress-making conditions in the early stages goes a long way to curing them before they take a firm hold. Try to stand apart from your particular worry, see it objectively as others might regard it and that way you will often be able to put your minor compulsions, obsessions and anxieties into perspective.

Over all those states of mind, listed above, hovers the self-induced, negative self-hypnotic suggestion that all is not well, that illness, misfortune and failure control your life.

The hypochondriac induces illness by self-hypnotic suggestions that this or the other physical symptom exists in his body or mind and that he is going to fall victim to some illness or other. This introduces the psychosomatic conditions already referred to. Sometimes it is inadvisable to pore over a Family Doctor Manual or to take too much notice of the health surveys that appear in the press from time to time.

Self-hypnosis will not heal or cure genuine organic disorders in cases where a doctor's advice must be sought. But imagined or 'self-created' pains, symptoms of disorders, 'heart pains', difficulty in breathing, when no actual physical cause is present, *can* be cured by self-hypnosis which directs the mind to refute the existence of those symptoms. If there is no real physical lesion or genuine ill health, the power of your mind can bring relief if your faith in self-hypnotic suggestion is positive and powerful enough.

19

Four Effective Auto-Suggestive Routines

If you suffer from recurrent sleeplessness, or you lack concentration, or you wish to give up smoking or cut down on your drinking, study the following four auto-suggestive routines, adapt them for your own usage and repeat them many times over. A self-hypnotic trance is not specially necessary in these instances but, if these routines are used during a self-induced hypnotic session, so much the better.

For Curing Sleeplessness

'From now on I will sleep well at night. I will go to sleep exactly ten minutes after putting my head on the pillow, *every night*. I will sleep round the clock until the morning. I will not wake up until 7 a.m. (or whenever). If I set the alarm, I will wake up just before it goes off. From tonight I will always sleep well.'

For Lack of Concentration

'From this moment on I will be able to concentrate really well on the job in hand. I will remember and be able to recall all I have been told, all I have read and all I have been taught. I will remember all that I see, all that I do, all that I hear, all that I feel, all that I touch. I will be able to give my entire mind to everything. Nothing will be too complex or too involved for my mind to absorb and recall whenever I need it.'

To Give Up Smoking

'From the very next cigarette I smoke, I will begin to realise how very nasty they taste. Each cigarette I smoke will start to taste even more unpleasant. My stomach will begin to feel uneasy, my lungs constricted and my breathing restricted. I will go on smoking, making these unpleasant symptoms persist until I can no longer put up with them. Then I will know I just do not wish to smoke another cigarette. I will not want to buy any nor will I accept any from anyone.'

To Cut Down on Drinking

'Drinking will very soon make me feel sick. I will begin to hate the confused feelings that over-drinking brings on. I will no longer enjoy any alcoholic beverage. Instead, I will like tea, coffee, orange juice, cola, any drink that I know will not make me feel ill or fuddled. I will know when to say 'no' when offered more drink. I will know that from the time of my last drink I will begin to feel fitter, happier, more mentally alert and less aggressive.

Does it seem too simple? Slightly naive? Each one is a proven formula used by those who really want an effective cure. Believe in them and they will work for you.

20

Face up to Fear . . .
Within Reason

Stage artists, big and small in terms of fame and fortune, emphasise the fact that they always suffer from an attack of nerves
(stage-fright) before going on stage. It is an axiom among artistes
on screen, stage or television that *not* to suffer from nerves before
an appearance is bad. To suffer from nerves is good for, once in
the studio or on stage, nerves vanish and the actors give even
better performances than if they had been bubbling over with
confidence.

To the outsider that may seem to be something of an affectation
– a theatrical pose, an inbred desire for dramatisation.

But it is only too true. Actors and actresses, to give of their
best, *do* suffer from genuine stage-fright, or nerves, before going
on. (I can well vouch for this because, for ten years, I appeared on
Saturday nights, as a stage act in a famous London Tavern and
each appearance was preceded by an attack of nerves, stage-fright
and trepidation. But, at curtain-up, on stage at last, this all
melted away and the joy and the pleasure of entertaining an
appreciative audience produced one hundred per cent confidence.)

The essence of this auto-suggestive, self-imposed, hypnotic
state of mind when going on stage, or before cameras is the firm
resolution to face up to the *fear* of going on. The 'nerves' say,
'Hold back, you may fail.' But the positive suggestions say, 'Go
on, you will not fail.'

And there is no failure.

By facing up to a particular fear and going through with it, the
ordinary man or woman can finally dismiss anxiety *of* the fear
until it becomes non-existent. The fears that face the average
individual are not as recurrent as are the stage-fright fears that
nightly face the stage artiste or entertainer. Fears that face the
average person are often just one-offs – an important interview, a
confrontation with a colleague a meeting with a loved-one after a

serious quarrel. Even a consultation with a doctor when bad news is anticipated can be regarded with anxiety.

Those are common, everyday fears with which many people have to contend. Visiting a dentist is a fear. Being interviewed by the Inland Revenue or the VAT man yet another. Facing disciplinary action in a professional capacity. Seeing a Bank manager for a loan. All these situations and many more that constitute our daily lives mount up in the mind until they become actual fears.

Not facing up to them magnifies them out of all proportion. The longer the delay, the greater does the fear become. Fears of the sort described are mostly in and *of* the mind. They are not physical fears that could be caused by fighting a house fire, nearly drowning, having a serious fall, being attacked in the street by a mugger. These are sudden and unexpected fears in which the human element has to be taken into consideration when there is no time for a self-imposed, self-analysis on the spot to help solve the dangerous situation. These are the genuine physical fears and are most certainly not merely of the mind.

Face up to fear, *but within reason*. That excludes foolish feats of bravado aimed at impressing friends. Or inciting street trouble by deliberate antagonism. There are many, many ways in which we can attract danger. Those are the fears we must not invite because they are totally foolhardy.

Phobias are fears and we have discussed them at length. The *mind-created* fears we have just outlined are genuine fears that have to be faced. And it cannot be stressed often enough that not facing up to them could make all the difference to your personal happiness.

Negative, self-imposed auto-suggestions that we 'cannot' must be exchanged for positive suggestions that we 'can'. The mind is just as capable of accepting the 'I can' premise as it is of accepting the 'I cannot'.

Job, of Bible fame said: '*That which I most feared has come upon me*'. And it had! If he had gone forth (as they say) and faced his fear, no doubt he would have been able to conquer it in no time.

21

Self-Hypnosis to Cure Stammering

You can cure yourself of a nervous stomach by 'talking it away'. Your digestion will get much better, provided you keep an eye on sensible food-intake as well.

You can create a facial rash through worry and anxiety. But you can also 'talk it away' by positive self-hypnosis that removes the cause of the rash which is the worry and the anxiety.

All functional, that is, not genuinely physical, aches and pains and ill-conditions can be 'talked away' in any of the states of self-hypnosis described. Real physical conditions must be referred to a doctor. *Remember that!.*

If you have a stutter or you stammer, there is bound to be a reason for it. Some people have a stutter because they are left-handed. Foolish parents and probably school teachers as well have forced the child to use its right hand rather than its left hand. This has set up a conflict in the child's mind, because the right side of its brain has dictated to it that it should use its left hand predominantly and this has seemed perfectly natural to the child. Outsiders, by trying to make the child use its right hand, upset the control of the left side of the brain and conflict arises.

It is totally incorrect to attempt to defy the laws of Nature as they affect that child. It can go through life writing perfectly legibly, using knives and forks, typing, drawing, painting, carrying out all kinds of normal, everyday work with its left hand, for the child's brain says this is correct.

But there are, of course, some other reasons why a person develops a stammer or a habit of stuttering.

A child may have unpleasant, even brutal parents. It may be unhappy in the home. It may be jealous of a brother or a sister. It may be saddened by seeing its parents having dreadful rows. It may be a child of divorced parents. Instead of becoming a bed-wetter, it starts to stammer. This, as with bed-wetting, is a silent protest against conditions, situations and absence of love, harmony and the feeling of being wanted.

Later, in adolescent and adult life, the stutter or the stammer persists for the reason for it has not been brought to the surface of the conscious mind from the subconscious mind, where the deep, dark secrets are stored forever. Elocution experts may be brought in to help the victim to overcome the incapacity to speak in a normal, unhesitating manner. The patient may well be told to open his mouth, to articulate slowly, to breathe deeply and so on.

But the stutter or the stammer will remain.

Because the basic *reason* for the affliction has not been thought of, much less brought to the surface, explored, explained and finally dismissed.

If you, reading this book, stutter or stammer, or experience hesitancy in speech when confronted by an awkward situation and do not know the reason for it, try this experiment.

When you are by yourself in your home start to sing a song that you know well. Sing it over several times. And surprisingly you will find you do *not* stammer or stutter through the words!

Still on your own, select a paragraph in a newspaper or book but, instead of starting to read the words, *sing* them to a well known melody or tune. Make the words fit the tune, even though you may well have to distort or break up syllables to get them to fit in. Sing reasonably loudly, articulating as well as you can.

The odds are that you will sing right through the paragraph, suiting it to the melody and *you will not stutter nor stammer!*

Make this a very regular daily exercise, in private.

After each rendition of the words stop singing and start to read the words in your normal tone of voice. As you do so let your mind recall and dwell upon the words as they sounded while you were singing them. Appreciate how steady the flow of words was, no hesitation at all. Let your routine be 'sing and say, sing and say, sing and say', many times over at each session.

Follow-up with a self-hypnotic session in which you tell yourself:

- *I will not stutter nor stammer.*
- *I can sing without a stutter or a stammer.*
- *Therefore I can speak without a stutter or a stammer.*

Repeat this 'sing and say' routine every day and follow it up with the self-hypnotic session. Whether being made to change from left-hand to right-hand caused the stammer or whether something else was the cause, forget them all.

If you can recall circumstances from your childhood that may have caused the stammer, tell yourself, during your self-hypnotic sessions:

- *Those circumstances no longer affect me.*
- *I can sing well, therefore I can speak well.*
- *I am not stuttering nor stammering as I repeat these suggestions out loud.*

Make it an important point to concentrate upon those letters such as 'P' and 'S' and 'T' that most probably give you the most trouble in pronouncing when they are the first letter of a word. Or an 'F' or a 'K' or an 'H'. In fact, the dominant letters and words with which you experience the *most* difficulty.

22

Self-Hypnosis by Tape

Some firms sell cassettes with recorded instructions for inducing an hypnotic trance-state and then giving auto-suggestive therapy that is listened to by the 'patient'. It is often explained that it is a good thing to have the cassette recorder on a bedside table at night and to switch it on and to let it run on until sleeps takes over. The auto-suggestions continue while sleep prevails and the suggestions are taken in by the subconscious mind. Upon awakening, the cassette will have run its length and the suggestions will have been absorbed and the 'patient' will resurrect them to order. His or her conscious mind will then start to obey the instructions given.

The somewhat impersonal voice of the recorded messages given by a man or a woman who is invisible, unknown and unidentifiable, may perhaps not register strongly enough with the participant in this therapy. The solution to this is to make your own tape which can be re-used many times over.

Think of the valuable and appropriate positive suggestions *you* can record, every one with a direct bearing upon your particular problems. You could possibly spend a very profitable hour, using the powerful 'We' rather than the 'I' attacking those problems in your life that most trouble you, giving yourself recorded auto-suggestions, *in your own voice*, that later, you can play over again and again. You can then listen to the 'We' affirmations that give you the comforting impression of sharing your troubles with your second self as has already been explained.

If you are able to sleep alone, set the recorder off at your bedside and listen to your second self telling you what to do and what not to do or how to overcome a particular problem.

If you do not sleep alone, allow regular times to be by yourself, to switch on and to listen to your recordings. Or use any of the self-hypnotic methods already explained and, switching on the recorder, *listen* instead of repeating the affirmations to yourself.

You will believe far more quickly your own affirmations and suggestions than those spoken by a complete stranger. And, of course, your positive affirmations will be chosen by you and directed towards *your* particular problems.

23

Action-Replay on All You Have Learnt So Far

Before progressing further, ask yourself these following questions in order to satisfy yourself that, so far, you understand what you have learnt.

- **What is meant by suggestion?**
- **What is the difference between auto- and hetero-suggestions?**
- **What is the conscious mind?**
- **What is the subconscious mind?**
- **What is the psychosomatic body relationship with the mind?**
- **What is the meaning of fear?**
- **What is the difference between functional and organic?**
- **What are the phobias?**
- **What is a phobia?**
- **What is the difference between introvert and extrovert?**
- **What is an acceptivity state?**
- **What is a suggestibility state?**
- **What is a conditioned reflex?**
- **What does post-hypnotic suggestions mean?**

Now look back on those sections of this book that have a bearing on all of these questions and check your knowledge.

Train yourself every day to strengthen your gaze which will help you to strengthen your powers of concentration. This, in turn will help you to strengthen your powers of inducing a self-hypnotic state of mind.

Train yourself,

- **by the 'staring at a given object' technique;**
- **by bathing the eyes with eye-lotion;**

- **by staring at a bright white light;**
- **by staring at the nape of the neck of someone and willing him to turn;**
- **by staring someone right between the eyes while talking to him.**

Transcendental meditators overcome stress by using self-hypnosis as a method of relaxation. The older you grow, the more valuable does this method of overcoming stress become as it helps eradicate the onset of psychosomatic ill-conditions. Even the conditions themselves in many proven cases.

In the next chapter, you will absorb some useful and effective auto-suggestions to use when you have induced a meditative state of self-hypnosis.

24

Suggestions While in a State of Meditation

A state of relaxation and meditation is induced by sitting in a comfortable armchair and placing your hands in your lap. Then join fingers and thumbs together to make an 'A' of your fingers. In this way you are completing a circuit of positive and negative elements and your mind is the 'lamp' you are now lighting.

Allow your mind to become completely drained of all thoughts. Close your eyes. Behind your closed eyelids you will see shapes and forms and colours, all in pleasant movement.

Concentrate upon the moving shapes. They will spiral and coil and come and go, sometimes developing into vague faces and figures. Keeping your finger tips and thumbs still forming the 'A', begin to say softly to yourself:

1 *All is peace and quiet. All is perfect calm. I am calm. The whole world is calm. There is peace. Perfect peace. I am now complete master of myself. I am relaxed and ready to receive calm, happy thoughts. They will banish all my worries and anxieties.*

Now begin to wish away your worries.

2 *My worries are vanishing – dissolving into thin air. Soon, they will no longer exist. Now, they no longer exist. I have no worries, no anxieties. I am an impregnable rock against all things that are worrisome to me.*

Now press your fingers and your thumbs together more firmly.

3 *Pressing my fingers and thumbs together I am completing a powerful circle of positive power that cannot be broken by anyone but myself. My entire body is now one powerful circle of resistance against all worry-thoughts. No one can enter this strong circle I have formed around myself.*

Begin to enumerate your chief worries and anxieties. For each worry brought to mind press a finger against the other finger to emphasise it. There may well be five worries, one for each of your two sets of fingers and one for your thumbs. They may be your home, your family, your money, your health. Pressing the fingers or thumbs together, concentrate on the entire anxiety-thoughts relevant to home, family, money and health in turn. Analyse and dissect each worry to the full, in every detail.

After some time spent on contemplating and meditating on each worry go through the list again, releasing the contacts between each finger and each thumb in turn as you say to yourself:

4 *No more home worries.*
No more family worries.
No more money worries.
No more health worries.

At the *end* of the positive auto-suggestion programme you have set out for yourself on the grounds just explained you will have moved your fingers and your thumbs completely apart, therefore breaking the positive-negative circuit and the 'lamp' that you have lit will now be extinguished. The meditative session will be over. Now tell yourself:

5 *I have broken the powerful circuit. All my worries have been extinguished. I am now completely free of all worries. I am peaceful and calm.*

You can, of course, use the 'We' personality rather than the 'I' personality if you so wish.

Transcedental Meditation was founded some thirty years ago by Maharishi Mahesh Yogi. Its main aim was, and still is, to cure stress by replacing that turbulent state of mind with a calmer state. Doctors and psychiatrists the world over now recognise the very real value of this self-hypnotic process, even in the curing of diseases to do with the heart, infectious diseases, tumours, disorders in the realm of mental medicine and afflictions of the nervous system. The process is usually carried out on the group-therapy system but can be equally effective when practised by the individual on his own.

The example just illustrated is an extremely simple, but nevertheless very effective routine. The technique of establishing a 'closed circuit' within your body and your mind by touching your fingertips and thumbs together, establishes a rapport within yourself that makes the auto-suggestive affirmations you make a great deal more effective. Pressing the fingers and the thumbs together adds emphasis to your suggestions; parting your fingers and the thumbs releases the stresses and the tensions which then metaphorically fly away from you as the body-mind circuit is broken.

A meditative system for developing your powers of concentration is equally as effective, but needs more mental effort on your part. It is, in effect, a technique that requires an alertness of mind rather than being a process of subduing the thinking processes. The method is as follows:

The Space Method

Sitting in an armchair clasp your hands together loosely and in a relaxed manner. Close your eyes and let your head rest back in a comfortable position. After a short while, start to imagine that you are looking deep into space. Paint a mental picture in your mind of the vast infinity of space, reaching far, far out into the Universe. The stronger your imagination, the more graphic will become the pictures in your mind, translated into visions that now start to flit before your closed eyes.

Imagine the miles rushing by you as you penetrate further and further into this infinity of nothingness.

When, finally, you really can persuade yourself that you are flying through space with great speed, tell yourself:

'I am flying through space. I have left the world way behind. I have concentrated my mind so strongly and with such determination that this has become a reality'.

Extend your fantasies as far as you wish. Clasp your hands together, tightly now, and concentrate hard on forcing pictures into your mind that evolve into actual visions behind your closed eyes. Dramatise the situation as far as your imagination will permit. Let your wildest imageries and fantasies take shape in your mind using the 'screens' of your closed eyelids to project the pictures onto.

Coming out of this concentrated effort may well leave you

mentally exhausted when you open your eyes again to the world and begin to relax.

This exercise, repeated at regular intervals, at your leisure, will have the positive effect of assisting you to concentrate powerfully and decisively on those things that most need your urgent attention in your business and working life. In a world where fiction is rapidly becoming fact in nuclear and space research the fantasies suggested should be easy for you to entertain.

A further exercise in meditation, this time with the purpose of inducing a state of balance in a crisis, we will call:

The Void Method

This is a variation on the Space Method but is intended to produce in your mind and in your body a state of balance and serenity. It is a direct opposite of the Space Method just explained, in which you were required to stretch your imagination to the hilt. Imagination is certainly required, but not in quite so forceful a fashion!

Here is the process.
Lie on your bed in a completely darkened room. If at all possible, no chink of light should be seen.

After a few moments start to think yourself into deep relaxation as previously described. This time, visualise your relaxed limbs float away from the bed, upwards, towards the dark ceiling. This is not the time-honoured astral projection of course, but a fantasy in your mind that it is actually taking place. Pleasant, but deep concentration will soon help you to feel you *are* rising up from the bed and floating in air near to the ceiling, which you cannot see. You are floating in a void surrounded by nothingness. You lose the sense of the support of the bed beneath your body, for now you are floating free in space.

Will your mind to accept that you *are* suspended in inky blackness, with nothing around you. You are floating in space. You are completely relaxed. Your body feels as light as air.

In this state of imagined suspension start to recite, in your mind, the positive auto-suggestive affirmations that you have predetermined before this session has started.

The longer you stay in this imagined state of suspended animation, the more detailed and brilliant will be the coloured images which will be floating before your closed eyes. As you mentally repeat each positive suggestion the words and the thoughts will take on shapes and forms before your closed eyes that will start to represent and to personify those words and thoughts. Visions of the faces of those who oppose you will be seen. Sharp shapes in colour will represent those pains and ill-conditions you want to wish away.

Allow yourself to enjoy these spectres of your imagination and, in your calm state of mind, let them soothe you, make you *feel* calm and serene as you float in space.

After a little while, open your eyes in the darkness and the wraith-like visions will still be there lingering in your imagination and as visual phantoms of the pictures you have seen while your eyes have been closed.

Finally, will yourself down again, onto your bed. After resting there for a moment or so rise, pull back the curtains or switch on the light. Your state of suspended animation and meditation in space will have left you feeling wonderfully relaxed and calmed, ready to face the negative things in your life that you have sought to dismiss.

Bear in mind always that in meditation and in all the methods of self-hypnosis so far described, you are *always* conscious. Always able to speak to yourself either out loud, or in your mind.

You are always *aware*, for you do not lose control of yourself.

Success depends upon dedication to, and acceptance of, the fact that you *can* hypnotise yourself in whatever way you choose from the methods you have learned. Have absolute conviction and a firm purpose to persevere, dismissing any personal embarrassment you may feel in leaving the normal run of things for brief spells to travel into the realms of fantasy. Escaping into a fantasy world from time to time has considerable therapeutic value. It enables the conscious and the subconscious to sort things out, to differentiate fact from fiction, positive from negative, hope from despair, joy from sadness. The result can be a positive mix of all those states of mind and body.

25

Self-Hypnosis and the Pain Factor

We have looked at the Indian Fakirs with their ability, through self-hypnosis, to dismiss thoughts of pain which enable them to walk on hot coals and to lie on beds of nails. Such a process demands a powerful and an intensive dismissal of thoughts of pain so that the brain just does *not* flash messages of pain to an affected part of the body.

Provided pain is not deeply rooted in a condition that needs medical or surgical attention, but is merely a functional pain brought on by some kind of anxiety then it can be soothed and wished away by the methods of self-hypnosis you have learned.

It is a matter of interest, in this context, to know that a few unfortunate people are born with a total incapacity to feel pain of any sort either self-inflicted or brought about by other sources. This condition is known as *congenital insensitivity*. It first becomes apparent in the baby or the growing child when its parents see it falling over and injuring itself with absolutely no feeling of pain.

Such a child may well bang its head against a wall, fall down stairs, prick itself with a needle, laugh instead of cry. It could lean against a hot radiator, burning the skin, but feeling nothing. It could hold its hand over the naked flame of a lighted candle and giggle with glee.

But, no pain would be felt.

This phenomena is brought about because the child's brain is unable to accept and translate messages of pain which are being transmitted to it by the nerve endings surrounding the area of injury.

No message - no pain.

There is no cure for this distressing condition. In adulthood such an individual would be incapable of experiencing pain.

This condition exists from birth and is brought about by one of two ways. The first is that the nerves that cause the sensation of pain are completely missing. In the second place the nerves, like a faulty electric circuit, are not correctly connected or 'wired-up' so that no messages of pain ever reach the brain to cause any sensation whatsoever. It is like an electric light bulb that is not connected to the mains so will not light up when a switch is pulled. There are simply no wires (nerves) leading from the source (a cut or bruise) to the lamp to light it up.

When, however, as is the case with most of us, our nerve-endings are correctly connected to our brain, we experience pain the moment we are aware of having injured ourselves.

It is of paramount importance *to* feel pain, for this is Nature's way of telling us to take immediate remedial action in order that the source of pain does not develop more serious aspects, and complications do not set in.

However, as has already been demonstrated, functional pains and aches can be soothed away by self-hypnosis provided they have absolutely no physical origin. You can develop *nervous* asthma, migraine, ulcers, spots, rashes – even temporary blindness, deafness, paralysis of the limbs, by the powerful negative suggestions from outside sources or by your own dreadful worries, anxieties and guilt-feelings. A trained psychiatrist can discover the root and the reason for these psychosomatic pains and dismiss them in the light of reality, commonsense and a realisation of their true origin.

Happily, we can do exactly the same *if* we accept that fact, act upon it, and believe in our own ability to cure ourselves!

Providing that all our nerve endings are correctly joined up and wired up to our brain, so we shall experience pain with all its warnings, in the normal manner. And in the majority of cases, this is so.

When we know for sure, by self-analysis, that the sources of these pains are merely functional and arising from negative thinking, then we can cure ourselves by continued and convinced self-hypnosis.

26

Seven Auto-Suggestive Affirmations

We will now deal with seven states of mind and body that can be treated, very successfully, by self-hypnosis or, in a less complicated form by the mere process of sowing the seeds of positive attitudes by auto-suggestion.

While self-induced hypnosis is helpful in every possible way in applying these seven affirmations, they can be as effective without a trance-state being induced when, for instance, it is not possible to be on your own. These affirmations can be sent to the subconcious mind at any time, under any circumstances provided sufficient concentration is applied while repeating them silently.

The seven states of mind and body with which we will now deal are:

1 **A desire for Bodily Strength**
2 **A desire for Self-Confidence**
3 **A desire to overcome the effects of a Bad Digestion**
4 **A desire to develop Clear Thinking**
5 **A desire to be able to overcome Fear-Thoughts**
6 **A desire to overcome Worry-Thoughts**
7 **A desire to Cultivate Courage**

The nervous system, consisting of the cerebro-spinal system, under the direct control of the brain, responsible for all voluntary action, and the automatic (involuntary) nervous system are both connected. Together, these are responsible for the absolute motivation of the body by the nerve-force. The automatic system which controls the heart, stomach and all the vital organs and their various functions, must always act in complete accord with the *nervous system*.

The function breathing is of paramount importance in dispelling negative thoughts and taking in positive thoughts or affirmations.

Breathing in takes in oxygen. Breathing out expels poisons. On that premise,

- **Breathe in and visualise those positive thoughts you fail to absorb mentally.**
- **Breathe out and tell yourself you are ridding yourself of all negative thoughts (poisons).**

Practise this often and your brain will react accordingly and your thoughts will soon become more positive.

While you should apply one or more of the following seven auto-suggestive affirmations first thing in the morning and last thing at night you can also apply them to yourself at any time when you can be alone.

At work, during your lunch hour, while in your car, in a bus or on a train, all are good times in which to apply the following auto-suggestive affirmations.

1 For Bodily Strength

I feel stronger every day. I can feel the good blood running through my veins. I have perfect control over my breathing. My legs feel strong as I walk. My arms are powerful. Because I now think more clearly and in a more positive manner, my body is automatically responding. Therefore with a stronger mind I also have a much stronger body.

2 For Self Confidence

I am confident in all I do and in all my associations with other people. I am sure of myself. I speak well, have a good personality. I look good for I feel very well. I know people with whom I associate like me. I am confident and can stand on my own two feet, make my own decisions, impress and influence others in my working life, my home life and in my social activities.

3 To Overcome the Effects of a Bad Digestion

I know that negative thinking, more especially at meal-times, upsets my digestive tract, poisons my bloodstream and therefore causes me to suffer from indigestion. I know that I must not let myself be upset at meal-times either by my own thoughts and actions, or by negative things I say to others or they say to me. I will not be faddy about foods for, if I suspect them, they may affect my stomach. But I will be particular, in a reasonable and a normal manner, about what I eat. And, when I eat, I will know I am taking in good, digestible foods. I know my stomach is strong since I am now eating the right foods. I will not hurry my meals nor allow myself only a restricted time in which to eat.

4 To Develop Clear Thinking

I have a crystal-clear mind. I can take in all I have to absorb and I can recall all I have learned in the past. My thoughts can prompt and promote immediate action when required with absolutely no hesitation on my part. I have good powers of concentration. Nothing can escape my agile mind. I am perceptive and clear-thinking. I am in complete control of my thought capacity. I have an index-mind and do not allow facts and figures to get confused or muddled up. I am able to remember names and recall faces. I can remember times, days, dates, data.

5 To Overcome Fear-Thoughts

I fear nothing within sensible reason. I certainly do not fear being afraid. I acknowledge a reasonable sense of precaution and self-preservation, but I do not permit that to make me create false fears of impending crises. I see all things in their correct perspective and therefore do not give way to irrational thoughts. I do not fear thoughts of illnesses based on negative states of mind that I know can poison my bloodstream and bring on false symptoms of irregularities of mind and body.

6 To Overcome Worry-Thoughts

I will not allow anything to worry me. There are solutions to all problems and I can find them. I will be master of everything that comes within my responsibility. I will not permit anything to get me down. Today is good and tomorrow will be even better. I have forgotten any fears I had yesterday. Most of my worries are in my mind and have no foundation in reality. But I will tackle very real worries and solve them as quickly as I can.

7 To Cultivate Courage

I have the courage of my convictions. I am aware of my many responsibilities and I know how to face up to them. I am a tower of strength and have the courage and the ability to face up to anything. I will not permit others to rob me of my feelings of courage, strength of mind and convictions and my total belief in myself. There is no reason why I should not have the courage to face up to anything and to overcome it.

Think these things to yourself often and say them to yourself in private. Breathe in and out as you repeat these affirmations on your own and when you can be alone. Make them be as powerful, as persuasive and as potent as the devoted believer makes his prayers.

There is no limit to the power of positive thought. Of all the many organs in our bodies we seem to pay less attention to the brain and the mind than to any of the other organs. But the brain controls, to a very large degree, our health and all the actions we take to create a happy existence for ourselves.

Therapy to Fight Your Nerves

We have 180,000,000 nerves! Quite an extensive network! We employ 18,000 when we just use our eyes in the everyday act of seeing.

Many people think they suffer from 'bad' nerves. A great deal of that is really bad thinking. Negative thoughts jangle the nervous system and, if people do not cancel negative thoughts by positive thoughts, nerves become more and more jangled so that short-circuits occur in many parts of the human body.

Nerves are a collection of fibres of which neurons are made. Neurons are cell-bodies with projections – conductors of the nervous impulse. As with the strings of a harp, a cello or a violin, they vibrate when 'plucked'. They are, in fact, tiny, thin fibres that are alarmingly alive and that receive and record most sensory experiences. They keep us aware of pain and of pleasure.

Nerves send messages to the brain. Without them life just could not be lived. In chapter 24 we explained the pain factor in relation to our nerves and the messages that are sent to the brain when injuries occur. Pleasurable sensations via the nervous system are also transmitted to the brain in just the same way and are demonstrated in feelings of warmth after coldness, tickling sensations and soothing sensations, the pleasures of imbibing hot drinks, cold drinks, enjoying food and so on. Also, of course, the intense sensations of the male and female orgasm are manifested by pleasure-messages received by the brain via our nerves.

On the negative side many individuals use 'nerves' as excuses to avoid responsibilities, confrontations, unfavourable work, upsetting surroundings, debts that cannot be met and many other situations.

It is all too easy to go to your doctor and to declare yourself to be suffering from 'nerves' as ample excuse for various psychosomatic ill-conditions that get sick notes, medical certificates and tranquilisers *ad lib*.

Genuine cases of real nervous disorders and nervous break-down brought about by very real crises or actual physical lesions must always be referred to a doctor who will recognise them as being really serious. Then appropiate medical advice and treatment will be forthcoming.

We are dealing, though, with the occupational disease of the discontented, the harassed and the anxiety-ridden subject who either genuinely believes nerves are at fault or who purposely takes refuge in the possession of 'bad' nerves in order to attract attention. It is like using the complicated network of the telephone system to relay false messages to a gullible public.

Manifestations of what we like to call 'bad' nerves are apparent when we are prone to fly off the handle time and time again at the slightest irritation. When tempers are lost at the merest excuse. When loud bangs and noises make us jump. When creaking doors jar on us. When there appears to be too much work to handle, too many decisions to make, too many people to cater for all at once.

A little thought and reflection would make us realise that it is not so much our nerves that are bad as our *thoughts* that are bad or negative.

If we have negative thoughts towards certain facts we attune our nerves to a non-acceptability attitude towards them. Our nervous system, dictated to in that fashion reacts accordingly and we, in turn, are affected.

Just think of what happens when our nerves are attacked and influenced by negative attitudes and the nervous system gets put out of gear.

- **Secretions in the salivary glands dry up (Dry mouth and throat).**
- **The stomach ceases to make hydrochloric acid (Stomach ache, gripes).**
- **The walls of the gastro-intestinal tract close (In-digestion).**
- **We can develop mucous colitis, among many other things already mentioned.**

If we do not start to change negative attitudes for positive attitudes when we allow our nerves to get the better of us the gastric juices begin to burn up the wall of the stomach and the mucous membrane Then, a peptic, gastric or duodenal ulcer can develop.

All are avoidable if we control our nervous output and input by controlling the false messages those same nerves send to our brain because of what we think.

It should be the simplest thing in the world to realise that our bodily health and our mental and emotional acumen is controlled by how we think.

The inveterate sufferer from 'bad' nerves who wilfully permits himself to cultivate them and to suffer from them becomes fearful. In chapter 20 we examined the phenomenon known as fear. Let us enlarge a little more on fear. It is behaviour dominated by an impression of things that are negative and unpleasant, accompanied by reactions of the nervous system that give rise to a desire for flight, that create trembling of the limbs, mental paralysis, physical inability and disability that prevent instant, positive action. As we saw in the chapter dealing with phobias.

Take a look at the following reasons *you* may have for thinking you suffer from 'bad' nerves. All general domestic and industrial 'happenings' in your daily life that bring you discomfort and cause your nervous reactions to bring on headaches, stomach aches, irritability, bad temper, confusion of thought and send a multitude of negative messages to your brain.

- **Your neighbour's radio or television is always too loud.**
- **You can smell something 'funny'.**
- **You have forgotten to turn off gas taps, water taps, electricity.**
- **You have not secured the windows, set the alarm, locked the doors.**

So you have to knock on the bedroom wall to shut your neighbour up. You have to get out of your warm bed to do the rounds of the house all over again to make sure that everything is, in fact, switched off.

Maybe you cannot go to sleep. A door somewhere is creaking. A dog is barking incessantly. Can you smell burning? Is your baby crying or someone in the family coughing? Is that a fire engine you can hear in the distance?

Many of those negative thoughts promoted by jangled nerves are paranoid in origin, because you think all those noises are aimed directly at you by unseen elements that are out to persecute you.

These paranoid impressions start to make you feel aggressive.
The more aggressive you feel the less likely you are to be able to drop off to sleep. Now your nerves are *really* jangled and upset and a confusion of negative messages is being sent to your brain.

And in the daily run of things you allow your 'bad' nerves to produce the following negative reactions.

- **You can't make quick decisions.**
- **You hesitate, procrastinate, prevaricate.**
- **You stutter and stammer. Words rush to your mouth but nothing is said.**
- **Your hands get hot and clammy in a crisis.**
- **Your mouth dries up, your stomach aches.**
- **You are sick or taken short.**

In regard to your health – your 'bad' nerves prompt you to:

- **look at your tongue in a mirror;**
- **look at your eyes for traces of anaemia;**
- **cough to test your sputum for a chest disorder;**
- **worry about the colour of your urine;**
- **wonder if that pain is around your heart.**

But don't let 180,000,000 tiny little thready, wriggling nerves ruin your life. If one nerve is pulled out of your tooth, the tooth goes black. It dies, in fact. Pull your nerves to bits and you, too, can be dead to the world of reason.

Let us be even more direct and list physical and mental conditions you can bring upon yourself.

Depression	Near to tears; over-emotional; easily hurt; sensitive; persecuted (paranoid).
Melancholia	Suicidal thoughts; hopelessness; inertia; apathy.
Tension	Excitable; incoherent; unstable; indecisive.
Asthma, Bronchitis	Clogging-up of respiratory tract.
Heart	Chest pains; pain down the arms; 'Wind' pains.
Stomach	Diarrhoea; nausea; vomiting; loss of appetite.

Headache   Migraine; tension neck pains; neuralgia; eye pains.

All those mental and physical ill-conditions can be brought on by allowing your nerves to become 'bad'. And 'bad' nerves are brought about by negative thoughts. And they can all be avoided by positive thinking which will allow your nervous system to function correctly and as nature intends it to function

So either under any of the self-hypnotic methods described or in a deliberately programmed session of auto-suggestive therapy, or both, convince yourself of the following truths.

It all begins in my mind. Everything begins with a thought. So I will sort out my thoughts and dismiss all negative ones. A thought can be an impulse. Good or bad, but I must dismiss the bad impulses.

If I think in a positive way my nervous system will also react in a positive way and this will allow positive messages that all is well to go to my brain. In turn my body will react in a favourable fashion and I will no longer have 'bad' nerves.

Invest in that positive auto-therapy many, many times until you begin to feel your nerves are strong and steady. *It will work!*

28

Replace Pep Pills and Placebos by Positive Perfection!

Many people are never *better* than when they are ill; and never more *ill* than when they are *well*. (If you can work that out!)

It just means that such people are never happier than when they are ailing. They are 'pale and interesting'. They become the object of pity and tea and sympathy from relatives, family and friends. Their worlds revolve round visits to the doctor and prescriptions for pills, powders, placebos, tranquillisers, antibiotics, vitamin supplements, pain killers, slimming or fattening foods.

Quite seventy-five per cent of these people who take their self-imposed illnesses along to the doctor are rewarded with delightful days spent in bed or lounging listlessly in front of the telly while the rest of the world gets on with the business of living.

These are the folk who tell themselves they are ill as an escape from work and responsibility. And because they tell themselves that they are ill they eventually seem to be so. Very often, after such a prolonged negative self-hypnoidal programme as that, they do actually become seriously ill, having brought on genuine ailments that were, in the first place only psychosomatic symptoms. The nervous physical conditions listed in the preceding chapter, plus many others, have finally been accepted by the body and the mind as genuine conditions. They are then beyond the reach of positive auto-suggestive therapy, for medical men have had to take over and no amount of psychotherapy or self-hypnotic therapy will restore good health once fiction has turned into fact.

You hear people over the garden wall, in the street, in doorways, in shops and supermarkets talking avidly and happily about their doctors, their prescriptions, their medical certificates, their operations, their pills and powders and all the essentials for self-induced illnesses. All are victims of negative auto-suggestion which is turned into positive auto-suggestion for the benefit of the malingerer. To such individuals sympathy is the very essence of existence.

But you know that if you do not wish to succumb to functional illness and indisposition there is no reason on earth why you should. Placebos are sometimes given, and this, to the patient, constitutes a positive hetero-suggestive affirmation from the doctor that they will alleviate ills. Although these harmless pills have no curative effect whatsoever, the patient soon feels better. He believes the pills will do him good, so they do, though they may contain no actual medication at all.

If you suffer from functional ill-conditions brought on by worry and all the small problems we have so far described there is absolutely no need for visits to the doctor.

You can be your own practitioner. Emile Coué's positive auto-suggestive affirmation: 'Every day, in every way, I am getting better and better' still stands good today.

You can do away with sleeping-pills, for you know how to induce pleasant slumber and deep sleep.

You can dispense with pep-pills for you now know how to create confidence in yourself and to develop powers of concentration. Pep-pills induce synthetically created conditions of peace of mind that eventually fade as a dose wears off and lose their effects entirely in the long run as your body gets used to them.

You now know that well selected and well thought out positive auto-suggestions can keep you in the pink of condition.

Because, in exchange for tranquillisers, sleeping pills and anti-depressants you can tell yourself,

- *I am in perfect health and feel fit and well*;
- *I never felt better*;
- *People prefer me to look and to feel fit*;
- *I can be well if I want to*;
- *I can't be ill if I'm feeling well.*
- *I can be well all the time.*

Use those positive affirmations every day – either in a self-hypnotic session or as you sail successfully and healthily through your day.

29

Tell Yourself – and It Will Be So

Let us dramatise a day in your life and think up things that may dog you throughout your day. Let's think of the most dreadful worries you may have upon waking up to face your day.

I look ill. I feel faint. My stomach aches. I feel dizzy. My breathing seems to be restricted. Is that a pain over my heart? I'll not do that job properly today. I'm going to forget all I have learned. Tonight I will have to leave that party early for I will feel so tired. When I do go to bed tonight after work and after the party I will not be able to go to sleep quickly. Maybe I will not even go to sleep at all. And of course, I will not be able to do justice to the dinner that's being laid on at the party tonight. My stomach will play me up at work and by the time I arrive at the party I will be all in and I won't have any appetite. Had I better stay away from the office today and that will give me an excuse not to go to the party . . .

. . . and so on and so on, according to your plans for that particular day and evening!

Now realise the new you by putting into practise all you have learned and face your day in this way:

I look fine. I feel perfect. I look good. No stomach ache, no headache. I can breathe perfectly. I'm going to be a success at work today. Everyone will admire and respect me. I will make no mistakes. I will recall all I have learned. I will stay at the party to the very end and I will eat everything that is put before me at dinner. I will laugh and dance away the hours and, when I get home, I will lay my head on my pillow and drop off to sleep right away. I am going to take everything in my stride and everyone is going to like me. All day. And all evening.

These positive affirmations personify happy living through a confident awareness that if you *will* a thing to happen, it *will* happen. And your forthright thinking and positive attitudes will influence others as well, and they will react favourably to you.

Of course, you will have to adapt those two dramatisations to your own life-style.

The art of happy living is to expect, with absolute confidence, that life can be and will be happy, if you will let it. Maybe that sounds a bit trite, given average everyday trials and tribulations. But it is *attitude* that counts for so much in dealing with those troubles on a daily basis.

Mostly every mentally well-equipped and physically-sound individual has some particular talent, ability or capability that should be realised and brought to the fore. People of either sex who wish to specialise in a certain area can, by use of the positive 'I can and I will' auto-suggestive idea, make full use of their specialised talent.

Very often, self-doubt creeps in to personal plans for shaping a happy and successful career and in deciding to make the very most of a specialised talent or ability.

In all the decisions you make to promote yourself consider the following axioms.

What You Tell Yourself About Yourself and What You Can Do is Right. . .

1 **if it helps you to progress;**

2 **if it hurts no one else;**

3 **if it makes you happier, and others happier too;**

4 **if it keeps you fit and well, mentally and physically;**

5 if it is honest and above board;

6 if it helps you to have a pleasant personality;

7 if it helps others to progress as well;

8 if its moral aspects are above reproach.

If you can truly accept that those eight axioms apply to you and to your ambitions and totally agree with your auto-suggestive ideas for personal progress, go right ahead as from now. Nothing is impossible within the range and the limits of your own personal abilities and talents. Discover what they are at whatever age you happen to be. Many, many talents go undiscovered for years until suddenly they are uncovered and a brand new life begins.

The Plus-Mind and the Minus-Mind

Many people are victims of negative suggestions flung at them from all sides in their domestic, commercial and social spheres by others who seek to undermine their confidence in themselves, and who contribute to failures, disappointments, loss of pride and prestige.

There is the husband or wife, and sometimes even the children, who try to make a spouse feel inadequate, a poor provider, a useless parent. There are in-laws and interfering relatives who try to upset domestic harmony and to discredit the wife or the husband, the mother or the father.

There is the works' foreman who bullies his workers; the boss who looks down on his or her employees; the racist who demonstrates prejudice; the manager who purposefully prevents promotion. There is the social club chairman who prevents election to the club. There are social committees who reject new ideas.

So much hetero-suggestive criticism and opposition from so many quarters!

And you could be a victim of such negative attack from one, some or even all of these protagonists!

With strength of mind and purpose you will, by now, have cultivated the ability to meet and to overcome all hetero-suggestions that are flung at you from all sides.

Let us recap, however, and remind you of all the negative hetero-suggestions that may well have been directed towards you by others who . . .

- **may be spitefully disposed towards you;**
- **may give you bad advice in order to disorientate you;**
- **may try to make you feel ill when you are well;**
- **may try to discredit your abilities;**
- **may try to discount your mental capacity;**

- **may try to disillusion you about yourself;**
- **may try to smother you in insincere emotionalism;**
- **may try to attack your most vulnerable mental and physical spots;**
- **may try to shape and form your personality to their own liking;**
- **may try to make you feel inferior;**
- **may ignore you in the home, at work and in your social life.**

You may well come up against embittered, disappointed, frustrated folk who have failed to make a success of their own lives and who seek to try to ruin yours as revenge for their own abysmal failures.

Some young and even middle-aged people tend to say negative things to those older than themselves in a well-meant but tactless and unfeeling way that can have unfortunate effects on their 'victims'.

They will say: 'You are not so young as you used to be. You must rest up a bit more. You can't expect to be able to do all that you could do when you were younger. You are getting on, you know.'

True, the years *may* be slowly slipping away, but there is no need for anyone to suggest that decline is already setting in! It could make matters worse. And very often does.

All these observations and criticisms of a negative nature start in the other person's mind. So why should you allow another person to attempt to influence *your* mind and put you at odds with yourself? Don't be influenced by what others say unless, of course, it is constructive and of help to you.

Tell Yourself, When Attacked By Negative Suggestions:

- *I refuse this suggestion;*
- *I do not accept this suggestion.*

Say it straight out to your protagonist. Then say it directly to yourself. Many times over. Either by using self-hypnosis or as an immediate auto-suggestion.

You have a PLUS-MIND. Those who attack you with negative

hetero-suggestions have MINUS-MINDS and you must reject their opposition at once.

By permitting negative outside suggestions to sway and to influence you against yourself you stand to lose dignity and faith in yourself.

All because of what others say to you.

Negative suggestions thrust upon you by unthinking, selfish, self-centred individuals bent on destroying your self-confidence can cause you to lose:

- **your money;**
- **your home;**
- **your job;**
- **your ambitions;**
- **your prestige;**
- **your popularity;**
- **your personality.**

Automatic acceptance of outside, negative hetero-suggestions can cause you to cultivate an incorrect attitude towards yourself. You will then anticipate similar criticism and negative suggestions coming at you from all sides. You will start to suffer from a conviction that you have let yourself down in the sight of others and that what they say about you is right. Accepting negative suggestions will tend to make you tense, stressful, fretful, and lead you to feel victimised. You begin to develop an acceptivity state to those suggestions and become hurt and a ready victim to self-pity.

As a result those individuals who launch their attacks on you are encouraged to do so more and more.

When you suspect that negative hetero-suggestion is about to be aimed at you,

- **protect yourself with an inner calm;**
- **turn a deaf ear; refuse and reject;**
- **let rational reasoning relax you;**
- **deny the hurtful effects of adverse criticism.**

Acknowledge that you are an entity in yourself. *You* command. *You* demand. You are uniquely *yourself* and no one can rob you of that individuality. Your positive thoughts, actions and words stem from *you* and you alone. Tell yourself that no outside influences can change your personality or impede your progress.

31

Be Impervious to Insults

Negative outside suggestions from others, particularly from friends who suddenly turn against you, can hurt you deeply if you allow them to.

Immediate, self-preserving positive action is necessary on your part when negative conflicts arise among those with whom you associate.

There is rarely time, in the face of studied insults, hurtful remarks or innuendos to let self-hypnosis come to your aid. But quick, defensive action on your part can save the day (and your face) allowing you to walk away with your pride still intact.

An immediate response to negative influences can be brought to bear in the following ways.

In The Event of Insult, Provocation or Challenge to Your Better Nature:

- **Do not accept it. Protect yourself with calmness from within.**
- **Walk away. Or talk about a different subject. Change the mood and tempo.**
- **Summon your reserves of will-power to avoid your temper rising.**
- **Turn a deaf ear. Refuse and reject.**
- **Relax, after a confrontation, as soon as possible.**
- **Let the soothing waters of rational reasoning calm you.**
- **Stay out of circulation until you have dismissed any negative doubts that your enemies may have put into your mind.**
- **Make certain you are still as positive-minded about yourself as you were before the verbal attack upon your susceptibilities.**

- **Remember you are a complete individual. No one can rob you of that individuality.**
- **Your thoughts, words and deeds come from you and you alone.**

Positive convictions sown into your mind by sound auto-suggestive therapy, every day of your life, can help you to overcome the deadly effects of negative suggestions aimed at you from all outside sources. People who attack you in that way are intent on wounding you emotionally and morally, disturbing your peace of mind, robbing you of your dignity, making you have doubts about yourself and your abilities and your hopes for the immediate future.

The part of you that persists in letting you be hurt by offensive remarks stems from the child within you. That child is within all of us, ready with tears in an attempt to gain sympathy or fight off opposition.

So many people are ready to be negative all of the time and are easy prey to those who recognise this weakness, and who play upon it.

You, however, *do not wish to be, and* do not *have* to be that sort of a person. You can train yourself, by the methods explained, to become impervious to insult and destructive hetero-suggestions. You can train yourself to inflate yourself and to *deflate* others.

You can convince yourself that you do not have a mind that can be moulded or easily influenced by others, particularly as you have your *own* very potent powers of influencing people. You just have to tell yourself that *that is so.*

32

Ten Minutes to Improve Your Day

We have already investigated ways in which you can suggest to yourself positive moves for improving daily routine upon waking up. Those auto-suggestions put into your mind as you eat breakfast or travel to work will prepare you for the day ahead.

Now, consider this *extra* routine, or use it as an alternative. Make up your mind, before dropping off to sleep that, the next morning, you will wake up ten minutes earlier. If you have now trained your mind to tell you just when to wake up, irrespective of your alarm clock, you should have no trouble in waking up ten minutes earlier.

That extra ten minutes of wakefulness will give you additional time to prepare for the day ahead.

Lie comfortably in bed and give yourself ten precious minutes to think, and to think *hard*. You are about to think yourself into a really good day.

Ten-Minute Think-In

I will make today far better than yesterday. I will grasp every opportunity for progress that I can. Nothing other than perfection will satisfy me today in my work. I will reach out to grasp those things that, yesterday, seemed to be just that little beyond my reach. I will assert myself far more than I did yesterday. I will make my personality felt by those people who matter to my progress. I will know just what I want and I will go all out to get it. I will make myself pleasant and acceptable to those people with whom I work. That way I will get them to do what I want them to do. When I go to bed again tonight I will know that today was one of my very best days.

With such positive and firm resolutions, get up, have breakfast and set off to your job.

Alternatively, you can use this Ten-Minute Think-in routine before you go to sleep at night. Your firm auto-suggestions will then be 'slept on' by your subconscious and will be even more firmly fixed by the morning and your conscious mind will then start to work on them.

You have, by now, accepted the premise that what you think so you are. You must now also accept that what you are governs what you do. And that this process all begins in your mind. Since you have now learned how to use your mind instead of letting it use you, you are well on your way.

33

Anxiety Can Make You an Addict

Anxiety over your problems will not be drowned in drink, go up in smoke or be overcome by sexual excess.

Those are three typical defence-mechanisms used by so many people who are faced with anxieties, worries and problems that seem to be insuperable.

Smoking, supposedly, calms the nerves. Drinking deadens brain-power, dulls the senses and creates incoherent thinking. Sexual sensations momentarily shut out reality with the primitive power of orgasm.

Being addicted to any one or all of those habits constitutes an escape from the present when excess turns them into addictions rather than just passing pleasures.

While you are struggling to overcome the problems that are weighing you down your ability to auto-suggest into finding solutions can be disastrously negated by:

1 **excess smoking which clogs up the lungs, affects your breathing and injures the mucous membrane of your nose (and that's to say the least of it);**

2 **excess drinking which hardens the arteries, prevents blood from coursing through your body in the normal manner and can lead to arteriosclerosis or kidney or liver complaints;**

3 **excess sex which robs you of physical strength, distorts the brain and generally weakens resistance;**

4 **excess eating which can make you sleepy (when you should be active) and overweight.**

Your brain, under such duress, can hardly be expected to send positive and powerful suggestions to your mind and hence to your body to take immediate, defensive action in the face of adversity.

However much you may try to kid yourself that your anxieties do not exist because your sense of responsibility is being cancelled out by drinking, smoking, eating and indulging in sexual sensation – *all to excess* – the problems will still remain unresolved. In just the same way an aspirin will take away a toothache for a while but the bad tooth will still be there.

When, finally, your problems *do* catch up with you, demanding instant action, you will be so mentally and physically depleted in mind, body and spirit that you will have no resistance left to help you handle them.

The longer you run away from attempting to solve your anxieties and worries the less likely it will be that you will ever find the right solutions.

You have, by now, learned how to be calm during or after a crisis; how to concentrate to the full; how to talk yourself out of harmful habits and how to stand up to people, all through the influence of auto-suggestion and self-hypnotic sessions. Excess drinking, smoking, eating and sexual indulgence are physical pleasures that please the body but can displease the mind.

The time for controlled drinking, smoking, eating and love-making arrives when you have used positive auto-suggestions to help you out of your troubles and you feel you are, at last, permitted these indulgences and are able fully to enjoy them. In those happier circumstances and conditions far less damage is done to the body, for they no longer personify *escape*, but *triumph* over obstacles.

The root cause of anxiety is invariably having to make one of two vital decisions that will be favourable to you: yes, or no; perhaps or perhaps not. Under self-hypnosis, examine, in detail, what would happen if the the answer is yes, and what would happen if the answer is no. Under self-hypnosis ask yourself if it is a question of 'perhaps', 'possibly', or 'perhaps not'. In the calm state of mind produced by a self-hypnotic session you will find the answer, because you will have weighed the pros and cons with careful deliberation.

Conflict creates indecision. Calmness can cure conflict of the mind. Deliberation under the soothing influences of self-hypnosis can create firm decisions.

You know this now and should believe it.

34

Self-Analysis will Reveal the Real You

During the many times you will now benefit from self-hypnotic sessions as described in this book, and from repeated auto-suggestive therapies, why not slip in a little self-analysis as well?

Self-analysis is you baring your soul honestly. A recognition of, and an acceptance of yourself, with determination to eradicate all negative characteristics and to exchange them for positive characteristics. This can only really be done successfully by sincere soul-searching, with no holds barred. After all, it's only *you* with whom you are dealing, no one else need ever know. But everybody will be surprised when, suddenly, out of the blue, you turn into a positive person, sweeping all before you in the realisation of all your ambitions.

In common with all mentally, emotionally and physically sound individuals you share these three things:

1 The desire for self-preservation
I must survive. I must live long. I must be well. I must not be ill.

2 The instinct for self-nutrition
I must eat, drink, exercise, sleep. I must eat the right nutritious foods. I must absorb the right vitamins and minerals. I must not be hungry. I must ensure there is enough protein in my diet.

3 The instinct for reproduction
I must have children.

You most probably accept those three instincts and desires for happy living and acknowledge them as part of your existence.

Having, then, established yourself as a human person with the correct directions in life in common with everyone else, now start your self-analysis, the results of which should prove of considerable value to you in your self-hypnosis sessions. The answers to all negative traits you discover during your self-analysis are curable by using the self-hypnotic methods described in this book, plus the auto-suggestion as applied to each individual negative trait.

- *Am I easily frustrated in my wishes and ambitions?*
- *Do I very often feel aggressive?*
- *Have I a superiority complex in my dealings with others that annoys them?*
- *Or do I suffer from an inferiority complex when dealing with others?*
- *Am I over-conscientious, born of anxiety that I do not do things correctly?*
- *Do I generally feel insecure, unsure of myself?*
- *Do I lack confidence in myself, or habitually mistrust others?*
- *Am I easily hurt by criticisms levelled at me?*
- *Do I suffer from a guilt complex over any matter, past or present?*
- *Am I compelled to do things over and over again?*
- *Am I filled with anxiety compulsions and complexes?*
- *Am I forever trying to hog the spotlight?*
- *Do I often take the line of least resistance?*
- *Am I given to jealousy, avarice, spite?*
- *Am I over self-conscious of my appearance?*
- *Am I vain, conceited, filled with false pride?*
- *Am I prejudiced against certain things, or certain people?*

With thoroughness and fairness, answer all these questions truthfully, adding to them any other character traits you know you possess which are of a negative nature.

Applying your new-found knowledge of self-hypnotic methods and auto-suggestive techniques talk yourself out of all the negative traits you may have discovered in yourself.

Leave behind you the complexes, compulsions, neuroses, inhibitions, frustrations, repressions. In fact, all the usual samples handed-out from the psychiatrist's gloom-kit!

Then go out and meet new people. Listen to good music. Read books and newspapers. Get out into the green fields and relax in the sunshine, in the green grass, with the trees overhead. See the brooks, the streams, the lakes and the rivers.

Self-hypnosis, auto-suggestion and self-analysis will, together, have revealed your true self *to* yourself so that, at last, you can be a free spirit in your own right.

Conclusion

The magical effects of hypnotism and self-hypnotism are as old as history, handed down from century to century, decade to decade, as an important technique for self-preservation, a way of relaxation, a route to individual peace of mind and serenity.

In the dim distant past primitive man, we learn, knew of the strange powers exerted by hypnotic suggestion, to self and to others. Now, happily, *we* know all about it. It is accepted by the BMA as a powerful and a valuable influence in medication, and the dental profession also acknowledges its very great value in dealing with frightened patients.

The best discovery of all, perhaps, has been the revelation that one can hypnotise oneself completely, without the aid and the possible embarrassment of a hypnotherapist.

Hypnotic-influences are perfectly natural suggestions projected to a patient by a hypnotherapist but they are equally natural suggestions when projected to your mind by yourself. A hypnotist cannot make a subject do anything, under hypnosis, or as a result of post-hypnotic suggestions, that goes against the morals or the principles of that subject. Neither can a man or a woman self-hypnotise him or herself to do anything in direct opposition to their accepted standards.

This book has shown you known, valued and well-tried methods of inducing self-hypnosis and has fully described the effects that can be obtained from using this strange but perfectly normal power that lies within all of us.

You can develop this power further to make your life even happier if you so desire.

We can be our own most formidable enemy if we do not learn how to control our minds so that we can benefit from powerful and influential auto-suggestions.

Because what we think controls what we do, and, so very often, what we do influences and controls what *others* do for us, self-hypnosis can assist the fight against the vagaries of life, helping to reject the negative influences of our oppressors and guiding us towards a happier, more positive and purposeful existence.

Glossary of Terms in relation to Hypnotism and Self-Hypnosis

This Glossary contains words you have come across in reading this book on self-hypnosis. It also contains some words and phrases not included in the book but which have a direct bearing on its general subject-matter.

ABREACTION   An emotional crisis or conflict relived by a patient in an effort to cure the trauma caused by the crisis or conflict.

AFTER-IMAGE   A revival of a past or sensory experience that can be summoned from the subconscious to the conscious mind.

AMNESIA   Loss of memory due to an emotional crisis that does not want to be recalled or the result of a severe accident that impairs and puts a block on the memory.

ANAESTHESIA   Absence of pain, either psychologically or physically.

ANXIETY   Fear of most things that give rise to problems that seem to be insoluble.

ANXIETY HYSTERIA   A conscious expression of an anxiety-state that goes beyond mere thought.

ASSOCIATIVE MEMORY   Process of recall by association of ideas.

AUTONOMIC NERVOUS SYSTEM   The nervous system that maintains vital functions of the body.

BEHAVIOUR   All that is done by an individual throughout life.

CENSOR   Impulses that are forbidden by the mind or which are made to appear to be different and therefore not the original taboo.

COMPULSION   Irrational behaviour a person is compelled to indulge in, in order to convince himself that a certain thing is true or has been done to his satisfaction. Behaviour that prompts repetition of an act until satisfied it has been done.

COMPULSION-NEUROSIS   Compulsive obsessive behaviour, sometimes an indication of guilt-feelings.

CONDITIONED-REFLEX   A behavioural response brought about by a stimulus that prompts instant action.

CONVERSION-HYSTERIA   A repression of any sort translated in terms of actual physical pain.

DEFENCE MECHANISM   A way of keeping a sense of pride by resorting to untruths and fictional utterances to cover up a deficiency or to disguise a real or an imagined thought or criticism aimed from an outside source.

DELUSION   An unfounded belief or conviction that refuses to accept all evidence that it cannot be true.

DREAM   Mental activity during the hours of sleeping.

ECSTASY   A feeling of exaggerated exaltation that can manifest itself in posturing and posing, irrational behaviour and extravagant speech. (Also Euphoria)

EGO   Referring to 'self'. The 'I am'.

FACULTY   The mental functioning of an individual. Reason and memory. Mental alertness.

FETISH   Something regarded with irrational reverence.

FIXATION   An abnormal and all-compelling fascination with a person or an object or a state of mind. Transfer of affections from one person to another. A fixed idea on a certain thing or aim.

FUNCTIONAL DISORDER   Physical disorders that cannot be demonstrated by an actual, real physical condition.

GUILT-FEELING   A sense of being sinful, real or imagined.

HYPNAGOGIC STATE   The condition when one is about to fall asleep or to wake up.

HYPNOGENIC   Objects used by an hypnotist or by a person with the aim of inducing an hypnotic state or trance.

HYPNOSIS A trance-state induced by suggestion. Applies also to a trance-state induced by self hypnosis.

HYSTERIA A psychic trauma that a patient has no knowledge nor recollection of.

LOGICAL THINKING Thoughts and consequent actions motivated by logic and common sense.

MAGIC The accomplishment of certain phenomena that rank above the normal limitations of human endeavour.

MEMORY The recall of events, conversations and general topics that have been experienced are now remembered in detail.

NEUROSES Functional disorders that include and involve various maladjustments of mind and body.

PAIN Messages sent from the brain to an injured part of the body to demonstrate it has been hurt. A directive from the brain to take immediate action to treat the injury. Psychosomatic pain is a false message from the brain about an injury that does not, in fact, exist.

PHOBIA An exaggerated and morbid fear.

RECALL The ability to remember and to recount a past experience.

REFLEX An immediate reaction and response to certain stimuli that has not been learned. An instinctive reaction without previous tuition.

REPRESSION An unconscious tendency to dismiss and to exclude from consciousness an unpleasant experience or thought.

SCHIZOPHRENIA An uncontrollable tendency to assume the personality of another person, invariably in direct contrast to the person who suffers from the condition. A 'split personality' can change suddenly from one character to another entirely different character.

SUGGESTION Auto and hetero. Auto influences the person who tells himself certain facts. Hetero influences the same person, but this time from someone else who has told him certain facts.

SYMPATHETIC NERVOUS SYSTEM A system which alerts and prepares the body for immediate action in an emergency. It has an influence over the visceral organs, the duct and ductless glands and the walls of the blood vessels. It is part of the autonomic nervous system.

TENSION-RELAXATION   The rise of tension before an event and the falling of tension after the event. The relaxation and the dispersal of tension and stress.

THERAPEUTICS   Psychotherapeutics deal with mental abnormalities with psychoanalysis, group-therapy, pathological conditions as opposed to medical treatment and surgical treatment. Often the two are combined to effect total cure in a patient.

UNCONSCIOUS MIND   Repressed ideas that are brought to the surface by hypnotism and self-hypnosis in efforts to cure repression and inhibition.

WISH   A method of getting satisfaction for an unfulfilled hope or ambition. A fantasy held in the mind before the ambition is realised – and also held in the mind after all hope has gone of fulfilment.

WISH-FULFILMENT   Satisfaction experienced in the dream-life, in day dreams, in fantasies of what might be.

YOGA   A system of contemplation and meditation practised by Indians and philosophers. Includes certain bodily postures and breathing routines which are capable of inducing self-hypnotic trances.

Further interesting and helpful titles from FOULSHAM.

MAKE MORE FRIENDS
The Key to Success
By Gilbert Oakley

A valuable self-help course book from a well known author who explains how it is possible to create the right image and make people respond positively. A friendly formula for success.

THE POWER OF POSITIVE THOUGHT
The Key to Attainment
By Gilbert Oakley

Another of Gilbert Oakley's excellent self-help course guides, in which he proves that positive attitudes *can* be acquired.

WIN THAT JOB
By E L Mayoh

A book that gives all the information needed to rise successfully above the competition — and to emerge as a winner.

WRITE YOURSELF A SUCCESSFUL CV
By Susan Stoyell

Clear and helpful step-by-step guidance for youngsters, taking the dread out of job hunting and showing that it can actually be *fun*!

SEXUAL SECRETS IN HANDWRITING
By Patricia Marne

The most surprising sexual traits are revealed, and with the author's expert advice you can learn to recognise them for yourself.

RAPHAEL'S DICTIONARY OF DREAMS
The Classic Collection of Dream Interpretations

Every imaginable dream is included and interpreted in this classical reference book with its easy-to-follow A to Z format.

REVEAL YOUR DESTINY YEARS
By Steven Culbert

A do-it-yourself astrology book that makes personal predictions possible, simply and understandably. No training is needed.

PLANETWISE
By Barbara Hill

Another excellent book enabling the reader to cast a PERSONAL HOROSCOPE without having to learn astrology. Almost 30,000 birthdates are included.

SEPHARIAL'S BOOK OF CHARMS AND TALISMANS

Sepharial explains how charms and talismans work to bring health and fortune — and how readers can make their own.

SEPHARIAL'S BOOK OF CARD FORTUNE TELLING

This new edition of Sepharial's famous book explains the classic art of fortune telling — using the modern pack of playing cards.

THE LAST WORD IN MANAGEMENT
By Rolf White

Impress others with your wit and wisdom. A unique collection of quotations, quips and sayings, and an invaluable reference book.

THE COMPLETE TRAINING DIARY
By James S Taylor

A complete training guide for athletes, runners and weight lifters, with well illustrated exercises and a diary section for every day.

BEST AMERICAN CARD GAMES
By David Duncan

The very best of the American card playing scene. Every game fully illustrated by sample hands and deals for extra clarity.

BETTING FOR PROFIT
By David Duncan

The whole spectrum of horse racing analysed in depth. Winning systems and expert advice. An excellent reference book for punters.

FEED YOUR KIDS A BETTER IQ
Francine and Harold Prince

A revolutionary eating plan with *healthful* versions of junk food, scientifically balanced to give kids all the essential nutrients.

PERHAPS IT'S AN ALLERGY
By Ellen Rothera

The chairwoman of the Food & Chemical Allergy Association offers new hope — and possibly renewed health — to allergy sufferers.

Opening doors to
the World of books

**Book Tokens
can be bought and
exchanged at most bookshops**